KT-527-843

EDINBURGH
ENCOUNTER

NEIL WILSON

Edinburgh Encounter

Published by Lonely Planet Publications Pty Ltd
ABN 36 005 607 983

Australia	Head Office, Locked Bag 1, Footscray, Vic 3011
	☎ 03 8379 8000 fax 03 8379 8111
	talk2us@lonelyplanet.com.au
USA	150 Linden St, Oakland, CA 94607
	☎ 510 893 8555
	toll free 800 275 8555
	fax 510 893 8572
	info@lonelyplanet.com
UK	Media Centre, 201 Wood Lane, London, W12 7TQ
	☎ 020 8433 1333. fax 020 8702 0112
	go@lonelyplanet.co.uk

This title was commissioned in Lonely Planet's London office and produced by: **Commissioning Editor** Clifton Wilkinson **Coordinating Editor** Jeanette Wall **Coordinating Cartographer** Andy Rojas **Layout Designer** Carlos Solarte **Assisting Editor** Alison Ridgway **Managing Editors** Imogen Bannister, Brigitte Ellemor **Managing Cartographers** Alison Lyall, Herman So **Cover Research** Naomi Parker **Internal Image Research** Aude Vauconsant **Managing Layout Designers** Indra Kilfoyle, Celia Wood **Thanks to** Glenn Beanland, Lisa Knights, Charity Mackinnon, Wayne Murphy

10 9 8 7 6 5 4 3

Printed in China

HOW TO USE THIS BOOK
Colour-Coding & Maps
Colour-coding is used for symbols on maps and in the text that they relate to (eg all eating venues on the maps and in the text are given a green knife and fork symbol). Each neighbourhood also gets its own colour, and this is used down the edge of the page and throughout that neighbourhood section.

Shaded yellow areas on the maps denote 'areas of interest' – for their historical significance, their attractive architecture or their great bars and restaurants. We encourage you to head to these areas and just start exploring!

Relaxing in the sunshine in Princes Street Gardens (p77), looking up at Edinburgh Castle (p40)

NEIL WILSON

Neil was born in Glasgow but defected to the east at the age of 18 and has now lived in Edinburgh for more than 25 years. While studying at Edinburgh University he spent long, lazy summer afternoons exploring the closes, wynds, courtyards and backstreets of his adopted city. Since then he has continued to enjoy delving into Edinburgh's many hidden corners, taking a special interest in the city's pubs and restaurants. Neil has been a full-time writer and photographer since 1988 and has written more than 50 guidebooks for various publishers, including Lonely Planet's *Scotland* guide.

NEIL'S THANKS

Many thanks to Carol, Jim, Jen, Guzzle, Keith, Steven, Tom, Christine, Brendan and all the other reprobates who have provided moral and financial (and occasionally physical) support during the arduous task of researching restaurants and pubs. A special thanks to Amy Hickman, Philip Ritchie and Steve Hall for their time and patience. Thanks also to the travellers who chipped in with recommendations, and to the various people I pestered for their opinions.

THE PHOTOGRAPHER

In the last 12 years, Will Salter has worked on assignment in more than 50 countries in Africa, Asia, Europe, Antarctica and the Pacific. He has produced a body of award-winning work that includes evocative images of travel, portraits and sport. He sees photography as a privilege, a rare opportunity to become intimately involved in people's lives. Will lives near Melbourne, Australia, with his family. See www.willsalter.com.

Our Readers Many thanks to the travellers who wrote to us with helpful hints, useful advice and interesting anecdotes: Linda Bogaards, Signe Larsen, Evelyn Witt

Cover photograph People at old pubs along Grassmarket in Edinburgh © Chad Ehlers/Photolibrary. **Internal photographs** p56, p94, p113 by Neil Wilson; p14-15 GLF/Imagebroker; p20 David Robertson/Alamy; p45 Scottish Viewpoint/Alamy. All other photographs by Lonely Planet Images, and by Will Salter except p22 Karl Blackwell; p19 Bethune Carmichael; p13, p24, p115 Martin Moos; p6, p17, p21, p63, p67, p82, p142, p145, p148, p149 Jonathan Smith.

All images are copyright of the photographers unless otherwise indicated. Many of the images in this guide are available for licensing from **Lonely Planet Images**: www.lonelyplanetimages.com.

>HIGHLIGHTS

THIS IS EDINBURGH

You can always tell the character of a place by the nicknames it has earned. Appropriately enough for the city that inspired *The Strange Case of Dr Jekyll and Mr Hyde*, Edinburgh has two contradictory – but complementary – names.

The Athens of the North, a name inspired by the great thinkers of the Scottish Enlightenment, is a city of high culture and lofty ideals, of art and literature, philosophy and science. It is here that each summer the world's biggest arts festival rises, phoenixlike, from the ashes of last year's rave reviews and broken box-office records to produce yet another string of superlatives. And it is here, beneath the Greek temples of Calton Hill – Edinburgh's acropolis – that the Scottish Parliament sits again after a 300-year absence.

But Edinburgh is also Auld Reekie, an altogether earthier place that flicks an impudent finger at the pretensions of the literati. Auld Reekie is a city of loud, crowded pubs and decadent restaurants, late-night drinking and all-night parties, beer-fuelled poets and foul-mouthed comedians. And it's the city of Beltane, the pagan May Day festival where half-naked revellers dance in the flickering firelight of bonfires beneath the stony indifference of Calton Hill's pillared monuments.

With so many sides to its personality, Edinburgh is a city you'll want to visit again and again, savouring a different experience each time – the castle silhouetted against a blue spring sky with a yellow haze of daffodils misting the slopes below the esplanade; stumbling out of a late-night club into the pale gold of a summer dawn, with only the thrum of taxi tyres on cobblestones breaking the silence; and festival fireworks crackling in the night sky above Princes Street Gardens.

Top Monuments atop Calton Hill (p73), the 'acropolis' of Edinburgh **Bottom** Visitors to the Edinburgh Festival Fringe (p25)

CONTENTS

THE AUTHOR 03

THIS IS EDINBURGH 07

HIGHLIGHTS 08

EDINBURGH DIARY 23

ITINERARIES 27

NEIGHBOURHOODS 32

>OLD TOWN 36

>HOLYROOD & ARTHUR'S
  SEAT 64

>NEW TOWN 72

>WEST END &
  STOCKBRIDGE 96

>SOUTH EDINBURGH 108

>LEITH & THE
  WATERFRONT 126

SNAPSHOTS **136**

> ACCOMMODATION 138

> DRINKING 140

> FOOD 142

> ARCHITECTURE 144

> GAY EDINBURGH 146

> KIDS' EDINBURGH 147

> VIEWS 148

BACKGROUND **149**

DIRECTORY **157**

INDEX **169**

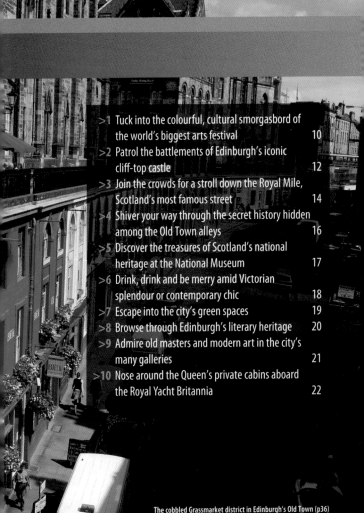

>1 Tuck into the colourful, cultural smorgasbord of the world's biggest arts festival   10

>2 Patrol the battlements of Edinburgh's iconic cliff-top castle   12

>3 Join the crowds for a stroll down the Royal Mile, Scotland's most famous street   14

>4 Shiver your way through the secret history hidden among the Old Town alleys   16

>5 Discover the treasures of Scotland's national heritage at the National Museum   17

>6 Drink, drink and be merry amid Victorian splendour or contemporary chic   18

>7 Escape into the city's green spaces   19

>8 Browse through Edinburgh's literary heritage   20

>9 Admire old masters and modern art in the city's many galleries   21

>10 Nose around the Queen's private cabins aboard the Royal Yacht Britannia   22

The cobbled Grassmarket district in Edinburgh's Old Town (p36)

>1 FESTIVAL CITY

TUCK INTO THE COLOURFUL, CULTURAL SMORGASBORD OF THE WORLD'S BIGGEST ARTS FESTIVAL

Visit Edinburgh in August and you'll find yourself caught up in a phantasmagoria of festivals. The Royal Mile becomes a colourful crush of people and performers, with stilt-walkers wading through the crowds and fire-jugglers' flaming torches arcing above a sea of heads. Jazz bands and majorettes parade along a packed Princes St, Charlotte Sq is transformed into a book-lovers' village, Princes Street Gardens is asprawl with sunbathers and picnickers, and the pub crowds spill out onto the pavements. The city's population almost doubles, and there is a permanent buzz of excitement in the air.

First held in 1947 to mark a return to peace after the ordeal of WWII, the Edinburgh International Festival is festooned with superlatives: the oldest, the biggest, the most famous, the best in the world. The original was a modest affair but today hundreds of the world's top musicians and performers congregate in Edinburgh for three weeks of diverse and inspirational music, opera, theatre and dance.

The famous Fireworks Concert, held on the final Saturday of the festival, is one of the most spectacular events of the year – a concert performed at the Ross Bandstand in Princes Street Gardens (and broadcast live on radio) is accompanied by the carefully choreographed detonation of around 40 tons of artistically arranged gunpowder.

When the first Edinburgh Festival was held, there were eight theatre companies who didn't make it onto the main programme. Undeterred, they grouped together and held their own mini-festival, on the fringe…and an Edinburgh institution was born. Today the Edinburgh Festival Fringe is the biggest festival of the performing arts anywhere in the world, but despite its size the Fringe remains true to its origins in three fundamental respects: performers are not invited to the event (they must make their own arrangements); they make use of unusual and unconventional theatre spaces; and they take all their own financial risks. The Fringe continues to be

one of the world's most exciting and innovative drama events. The sheer variety of shows on offer is just staggering – everything from performance poetry to chainsaw-juggling.

But it's not just in summer that the city puts on its party frock. Midwinter is also the season to be jolly, with a month's worth of festivities leading up to Christmas and New Year. There are Christmas markets with stalls serving glühwein (mulled wine), big-name bands playing live in Princes Street Gardens, and a spectacular torchlight procession down The Mound.

For more details see p23.

>2 EDINBURGH CASTLE

PATROL THE BATTLEMENTS OF EDINBURGH'S ICONIC CLIFF-TOP CASTLE

The brooding, black crags of Castle Rock, shouldering above Princes Street Gardens, are the very reason for Edinburgh's existence. This rocky hill – the glacier-worn stump of an ancient volcano – was the most easily defended hilltop on the invasion route between England and central Scotland. Crowning the crag with a picturesque profusion of battlements, Edinburgh Castle is now Scotland's most popular pay-to-enter tourist attraction, pulling in more than a million visitors a year.

You could easily spend the better part of a day exploring the multifarious attractions, from museums and militaria to chapels, can-nons, vaults and prisons, but don't miss the Royal Palace, built during the 15th and 16th centuries, where a series of historical tableaux leads to a strongroom housing the Honours of Scotland. The crown (made in 1540 from the gold of Robert the Bruce's 14th-century coronet), sword and sceptre are the oldest surviving crown jewels in Europe, and were locked away following the Act of Union in 1707 and forgotten until they were unearthed by Sir Walter Scott in 1818. Also on display here is the Stone of Destiny (see p40).

Across the square is the Great Hall, built for King James IV (r 1488–1513) as a ceremonial hall and used as a meeting place for the Scot-tish Parliament until 1639. It's crammed with swords and armour, but don't forget to look up at its most remarkable feature, the original 16th-century hammer-beam roof.

Also well worth a visit are the castle vaults beneath the Great Hall, which were used variously as storerooms, bakeries and prisons. The vaults have been restored as 18th- and early-19th-century prisons, where original graffiti carved by French and American prisoners can be seen on the ancient wooden doors.

At the highest point of Castle Rock is the tiny St Margaret's Chapel, the oldest surviving building in Edinburgh. It's a simple Romanesque structure that was probably built by David I or Alexander I in memory of their mother Queen Margaret sometime around 1130. Outside is Mons Meg, a giant 15th-century siege gun that was last fired in 1681

as a birthday salute for the future King James James VII of Scotland/II of England, when its barrel burst. Take a peek over the wall to the north of the chapel and you'll see a charming little garden that was used as a pet cemetery for officers' dogs.

If you time your visit right, you'll get the chance to stick your fingers in your ears as Sgt James Shannon (aka Shannon the Cannon) triggers the One O'Clock Gun (p78), a gleaming 105mm filed gun that fires an ear-splitting time signal at 1pm every day except Sundays, Christmas Day and Good Friday.

For details on visiting the castle, see p40.

HIGHLIGHTS

>3 THE ROYAL MILE

JOIN THE CROWDS FOR A STROLL DOWN THE ROYAL MILE, SCOTLAND'S MOST FAMOUS STREET

Quirky, colourful and crammed with attractions, Edinburgh's oldest street unrolls in a picturesque, cobblestoned ribbon from Edinburgh Castle downhill to the Palace of Holyroodhouse. Lined with pubs, shops and historic buildings, and surrounded by a maze of medieval wynds and closes, it sports a carnival atmosphere in festival time (p23) when the pedestrianised central section is crowded with tourists and performers.

Hemmed in for much of its gently snaking length with tall, 17th- to 19th-century tenement buildings, the Royal Mile is actually a mile plus 107 yards in length. The 'Royal' comes from being used by past kings and queens as a processional route between castle, parliament and palace, and it retains a grand, baronial atmosphere (the architecture was impressive enough to be remarked upon by Daniel Defoe, author of *Robinson Crusoe*, during a visit in 1723 when he described the Royal Mile as 'the largest, longest and finest street for buildings and number of inhabitants, not only in Britain, but in the world').

There are four named sections: Castlehill, Lawnmarket, High St and Canongate. A corruption of 'Landmarket', Lawnmarket takes its name from the large cloth market (selling goods from the land outside the city) that flourished here until the 18th century; this was the poshest part of the Old Town, where many of its most distinguished citizens made their homes (see Gladstone's Land, p42).

High St, dominated by the medieval crown spire of St Giles Cathedral (p46), is the heart and soul of the Old Town, home to the law courts, the city chambers and – until 1707 – the Scottish Parliament (see Parliament Hall, p46). Across from St Giles is the entrance to the haunted underworld of Real Mary King's Close (p46), while further downhill is the 16th-century house of John Knox (p44).

Canongate – the section between the Netherbow and Holyrood – takes its name from the Augustinian canons (monks) of Holyrood Abbey (p67). From the 16th century it was home to aristocrats attracted to the nearby Palace of Holyroodhouse (p68); today, it is home to Edinburgh's most controversial work of modern architecture, the Scottish Parliament Building (p69).

The ideal way to round off a stroll down the Mile from castle to palace is to hike up to the summit of Arthur's Seat (p66), or along Radical Rd at the foot of Salisbury Crags, for a brilliant view over the city.

>4 HAUNTED EDINBURGH

SHIVER YOUR WAY THROUGH THE SECRET HISTORY HIDDEN AMONG THE OLD TOWN ALLEYS

Edinburgh's least visible tourist attraction is the labyrinth of subterranean vaults, chambers and corridors that lies beneath the Old Town streets. As the city expanded in the late 18th century South Bridge and George IV Bridge were built southwards from the Royal Mile over the deep valley of the Cowgate, supported on underground vaults originally used as storerooms, workshops and drinking dens. As the population swelled, the dark, dripping chambers were given over to slum accommodation and abandoned to poverty, filth and crime.

The South Bridge vaults were cleared in the late 19th century and forgotten until 1994 when they were opened to tours. Certain chambers are said to be haunted; one in particular has been extensively investigated by paranormal researchers. There's also Real Mary King's Close (p46), a ghost-ridden time capsule beneath the City Chambers.

Other ghostly apparitions are said to stalk the Old Town's streets, wynds and cemeteries; the so-called MacKenzie Poltergeist in Greyfriars Kirkyard (p43) is the best-documented case of poltergeist activity ever studied. Whether the phenomenon is truly paranormal or just some sort of psychological effect remains to be seen. Meanwhile, ghost-tour customers are queuing up to scare themselves silly.

For details, see p161.

>5 NATIONAL MUSEUM OF SCOTLAND

DISCOVER THE TREASURES OF SCOTLAND'S NATIONAL HERITAGE AT THE NATIONAL MUSEUM

The modern Museum of Scotland, opened in 1998, is one of the city's most distinctive landmarks, and the imaginative interior design is an attraction in itself. Its five levels chart the history of Scotland from geological beginnings to the present day, with many imaginative exhibits, and audio guides are available in several languages. Highlights include the Monymusk Reliquary, a tiny silver casket dating from 750, which is said to have been carried into battle with Robert the Bruce at Bannockburn in 1314; the Lewis Chessmen, a set of charming 12th-century chess pieces made from walrus ivory; and the Ways of Death exhibit, a Goth's paradise of jet jewellery, mourning bracelets made from human hair, and eight of the 17 tiny coffins discovered on the slopes of Arthur's Seat in 1836 (see p68). Don't forget to take the lift to the roof terrace for a fantastic view of the castle.

The Museum of Scotland connects with the Victorian Royal Museum, dating from 1861, where the stolid, grey exterior gives way to a bright and airy glass-roofed atrium. It has an eclectic collection covering natural history, archaeology, scientific and industrial technology, and the decorative arts of ancient Egypt, China, Japan, Korea and the West.

For more details, see p44.

>6 TRADITIONAL PUBS & TRENDY BARS

DRINK, DRINK AND BE MERRY AMID VICTORIAN SPLENDOUR OR CONTEMPORARY CHIC

Despite nurturing a nascent cafe society with its regular summer blossoming of outdoor tables, Edinburgh is still deeply immersed in its pub culture. A drinker's town par excellence, with more bars per person than London and lots of late-night drinking dens, the Scottish capital offers a dazzling choice of venues for a night of revelry.

At one end of the city's broad spectrum of hostelries lies the traditional 19th-century bar with much of its original Victorian decoration intact, serving cask-conditioned real ales and a staggering range of malt whiskies – check out the colourful ceramic portraits at the Café Royal Circle Bar (p90), the polished brass and mahogany of the Abbotsford (p89), or the stained glass and mirrors at Bennet's Bar (p121; pictured above).

At the other end of the spectrum is the modern 'style bar', with a cool clientele, DJs on tap, and styling so sharp you could cut yourself on it. The staff here are more likely to be serving cocktails than pints – slide onto a sofa at Sygn (p106), Amicus Apple (p89) or Tonic (p93) for a taste of contemporary capital chic.

>7 GREEN SPACES

ESCAPE INTO THE CITY'S GREEN SPACES

One of Edinburgh's big attractions is the way the surrounding countryside seems to have insinuated itself into the very heart of the city. From the vast expanse of Holyrood Park with its miniature mountain, Arthur's Seat (p66), to tiny, hidden, green spaces such as Dunbar's Close Garden (p40), you're never very far away from a refreshing breath of country air.

As well as enjoying groomed and manicured parkland, like the city-centre jewel of Princes Street Gardens (p77; pictured above) and the exotic elegance of the Royal Botanic Garden (p98), you can escape to the wooded glades of the Water of Leith (p99), a haunt of otters and kingfishers just yards from the formal streets and squares of the New Town, or the picturesque glen of the River Almond at Cramond village (p128), or follow the wildlife corridor of the Union Canal (p112) running all the way from Tollcross to the edge of the city and beyond.

>8 LITERARY EDINBURGH

BROWSE THROUGH EDINBURGH'S LITERARY HERITAGE
Some of the most imposing monuments in Edinburgh are dedicated to poets and novelists, from the unmissable Scott Monument (p78) in Princes Street Gardens to the elegant Burns Monument on Calton Hill (p73). The city has nurtured and inspired literary talent from the days of Burns, Scott and Robert Louis Stevenson, whose lives are celebrated in the Writers' Museum (p48; pictured above), to the present day. Walk into Waterstone's (p82) or Blackwell's Bookshop (p49) and you'll find a healthy Scottish fiction section, its shelves bulging with works by bestselling Edinburgh authors such as Christopher Brookmyre, Quintin Jardine, Ian Rankin, Alexander McCall Smith and Irvine Welsh. Many have used the city as a setting; for our choice of top Edinburgh novels see p156.

The city also offers the pleasure of browsing at second-hand bookstores like West Port Books (p116) and McNaughtan's (p80), and specialist shops such as Word Power (p117). And don't miss the chance to mix books and beer on the highly recommended Edinburgh Literary Pub Tour (p161).

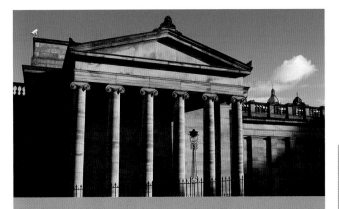

>9 ART GALLERIES
ADMIRE OLD MASTERS AND MODERN ART IN THE CITY'S MANY GALLERIES

As a capital city, it's hardly surprising that Edinburgh is home to some of the country's most important art collections. You can admire the old masters, from Titian to Turner, as well as Canova's famous marble sculpture of the *Three Graces,* at the National Gallery of Scotland (p76; pictured above), though for our money the painting that really catches your eye is the gorgeous portrait of *Lady Agnew of Lochnaw* by John Singer Sargent, with its barely repressed erotic charge.

The Scottish National Gallery of Modern Art (p98) and its near neighbour the Dean Gallery (p98) are well worth seeking out, not only for their displays of 20th-century art with works by Matisse, Picasso, Magritte, Mondrian and Giacometti, but for their beautiful setting in parklike grounds dotted with sculptures by Henry Moore, Barbara Hepworth and Eduardo Paolozzi, and graced with a seductive piece of landscape art by Charles Jencks.

And don't forget to check out the latest exhibitions of contemporary art at the Fruitmarket Gallery (p41), plus cutting-edge works by up-and-coming artists at the Collective (p40).

>10 ROYAL YACHT BRITANNIA

NOSE AROUND THE QUEEN'S PRIVATE CABINS ABOARD THE ROYAL YACHT BRITANNIA

The Britannia served as the royal family's floating home during their foreign travels until she was decommissioned in 1997. Now permanently moored at Ocean Terminal, the ship offers an intriguing insight into the Queen's private tastes. A monument to 1950s decor, the accommodation reveals Her Majesty's preference for simple, unfussy surroundings – the Queen's own bed is surprisingly tiny and plain.

There was nothing simple or unfussy about the running of the ship, though. When the Queen travelled, along with her went 45 members of the royal household, five tonnes of luggage and a Rolls-Royce that was carefully squeezed into a specially built garage on deck. The decks were scrubbed daily, but all work near the royal accommodation was carried out in complete silence and had to be finished by 8am. A thermometer was kept in the Queen's bathroom to make sure that the water was the correct temperature, and when in harbour one yachtsman was charged with ensuring that the angle of the gangway never exceeded 12 degrees. And note the mahogany windbreak that was added to the balcony deck in front of the bridge – it was put there to stop wayward breezes from blowing up skirts and inadvertently revealing the Royal Undies.

For details on visiting, see p128.

>EDINBURGH DIARY

Since the first Edinburgh International Festival of Music and Drama in 1947 the city has grown into one of the biggest party venues in the world, with a crowded calendar of contrasting festivals ranging from science and storytelling to movies and marching military bands.

Peak season is August, when half a dozen festivals – including the huge Edinburgh International Festival and the even bigger Festival Fringe – run concurrently, closely followed by late December, when the Christmas festival runs into the Hogmanay celebrations. You can find details of Edinburgh's main festivals on www.edinburgh-festivals.com.

Performers go head over heels for Edinburgh during the Festival Fringe (p25)

APRIL

Edinburgh International Science Festival

www.sciencefestival.co.uk
From dinosaurs and ghosts to alien life forms, the Science Festival covers a wide range of subjects with lectures, exhibitions, demonstrations, guided tours and interactive experiments. It runs over 10 days in late March to early April.

Beltane

www.beltane.org
Beltane is a pagan fire festival marking the end of winter and the rebirth of spring. It was resurrected in modern form in 1988 and is celebrated annually on the summit of Calton Hill. Held annually on the night of 30 April.

MAY

International Children's Festival

www.imaginate.org.uk
Britain's biggest festival of performing arts for children has events suitable for kids from three to 12.

JUNE

Edinburgh International Film Festival

www.edfilmfest.org.uk
This two-week showcase for new British and European films has moved its dates from August to June, starting in 2008.

Royal Highland Show

www.royalhighlandshow.org
Hugely popular agricultural show, a four-day feast of all things rural with everything from tractor-driving to falconry; held over a long weekend (Thursday to Sunday) in late June.

Contemplating a hands-on exhibit at the Edinburgh International Science Festival

Working hard for applause at the Edinburgh Festival Fringe

JULY

Edinburgh International Jazz & Blues Festival

www.edinburghjazzfestival.com

The festival kicks off with a Mardi Gras street parade and an afternoon of free music. Runs for nine days, beginning on the last Friday in July.

AUGUST

Edinburgh Military Tattoo

www.edintattoo.co.uk

A spectacular display of military marching bands, massed pipes and drums, acrobats, cheerleaders and motorcycle display teams played out in front of the magnificent backdrop of the floodlit castle.

Edinburgh Festival Fringe

www.edfringe.com

The biggest festival of the performing arts anywhere in the world; takes place over three and a half weeks in August, the last two weeks overlapping with the Edinburgh International Festival.

Edinburgh International Festival

www.eif.co.uk

The world's top musicians and performers congregate in Edinburgh for three weeks of diverse music, opera, theatre and dance; ends on the first Saturday in September. The programme is usually available from April.

Edinburgh International Book Festival

www.edbookfest.co.uk

A fun fortnight of talks, readings, debates, lectures, book signings and meet-the-author events; usually held during the first two weeks of the Edinburgh International Festival.

SEPTEMBER

Edinburgh Mela
www.edinburgh-mela.co.uk
Founded by the city's Bangladeshi, Indian and Pakistani communities back in 1995, the Mela is a weekend of multicultural music, dance, food and fashion, with plenty of children's activities. Held late August or early September in Pilrig Park.

OCTOBER

Scottish International Storytelling Festival
www.scottishstorytellingcentre.co.uk
An annual celebration of the art of spinning a yarn. Events for all ages staged at a variety of indoor and outdoor venues, leavened with traditional music and crafts workshops. Runs over 10 days, ending on the first Sunday in November.

WHAT'S THE SKINNY?
Long-established listings mag *The List* now has some competition in the form of *The Skinny* (www.skinnymag.co.uk). All the info in the monthly mag, which covers music, clubbing, visual arts, film, theatre, books, LGBT and comedy, is also available online.

DECEMBER

Edinburgh's Christmas
www.edinburghschristmas.com
The three weeks before Christmas see a fairground, Ferris wheel, German market and open-air ice rink in Princes Street Gardens.

Edinburgh's Hogmanay
www.edinburghshogmanay.com
The biggest winter festival in Europe, with a torchlight procession, live bands and a huge street party; events run from 29 December to 1 January. To get into the main party area in the city centre after 8pm on 31 December you'll need a ticket – book well in advance.

ITINERARIES

Edinburgh's compact city centre makes it easy to cover a lot of ground in a short time, but whether you're here for a day or a long weekend, our recommended itineraries will help you make the most of your time.

ONE DAY
Edinburgh Castle (p12) is Scotland's number-one tourist sight, so visit here first then take a leisurely stroll down the Royal Mile (p14), stopping off at any of the attractions that take your fancy. At the bottom of the hill, visit the public gallery at the Scottish Parliament Building (p69) or the Palace of Holyroodhouse (p68). In the afternoon take a look around the National Museum of Scotland (p17) and then, if the weather's fine, take an evening stroll up Calton Hill (p73). Round off the day with dinner at a restaurant with a view – the Forth Floor Restaurant & Brasserie (p85) or Oloroso (p87).

TWO DAYS
Follow the one-day itinerary then spend morning number two down at Leith with breakfast/brunch at Diner 7 (p132) or Café Truva (p131), followed by a visit to the Royal Yacht Britannia (p22). In the afternoon, soak up some culture at the National Gallery of Scotland (p76) or indulge in some shopping in the New Town (p79). Relax with a pint at the Guildford Arms (p91) or Café Royal (p90), or sip cocktails at Amicus Apple (p89) or Tonic (p93), then take a ghost tour (p161) before a late dinner at Maxie's Bistro (p55) or Maison Bleue (p55).

THREE DAYS
Fingers crossed and hope for good weather – begin your third day with a walk through Stockbridge to the Royal Botanic Garden (p98), or along the Water of Leith to the Scottish National Gallery of Modern Art (p98). After lunch at garden or gallery, take a bus to the edge of the city – depending on your tastes, head for the seaside at Queensferry (p129) or to the *Da Vinci Code* delights of Rosslyn Chapel (p112). Back in town, grab a pre-theatre dinner at Blue (p102) or the Tower (p57), followed by

---

Top The Palace of Holyroodhouse (p68) is fit for a queen **Bottom left** Stopping for a drink along the Royal Mile (p14) **Bottom right** It's all about the details at the stylish new Scottish Parliament Building (p69)

FORWARD PLANNING

Most trips to Edinburgh don't need much planning – just turn up and do what you want. The big exception is the Festival (p25); if you intend to visit during August, then you ought to get at least your accommodation sorted as far in advance as possible – a year ahead isn't too early. It's a good idea to book tickets for potential sell-out shows too (including the Military Tattoo), especially for weekend performances. The programme for the Edinburgh International Festival (www.eif.co.uk) is usually available from April; the Fringe (www.edfringe.com) programme is released in early June. You can order or download programmes online.

If you're planning to visit at Hogmanay (p26), remember that free passes for the city-centre street party get snapped up quickly. They are usually released at the beginning of October; a proportion are available online (register at www.edinburghshogmanay.com) from late September.

The other big occasions that are worth thinking about in advance are rugby internationals. If you're planning a quiet, romantic weekend in winter, it might be worth checking the match fixtures on www.rbs6nations.com to make sure you won't be sharing the city with tens of thousands of hard-drinking rugby fans. Accommodation will also be booked up well in advance for rugby weekends.

a play at the Traverse Theatre (p107) or a musical show at the Edinburgh Festival Theatre (p124).

RAINY DAYS

Edinburgh offers several indoor options where you can pleasantly while away a wet afternoon. Culture vultures will find plenty to keep themselves interested at the National Gallery of Scotland (p76), and can then walk dry-shod through the underground Weston Link to the nearby Royal Scottish Academy (p78); from there it's a quick dash across Princes St to Jenners department store (p80). If your tastes are less highbrow, take a bus to Ocean Terminal (p131) in Leith, the city's biggest shopping centre, which has a covered connection to the Royal Yacht Britannia (p22). Alternatively, you could bar-hop along Rose St or the Royal Mile (p14).

FOR FREE

They say the best things in life are free, and one of the best things about Edinburgh – its sheer beauty – is free for all to enjoy. You don't have to buy a ticket for the castle to take in the views from the Esplanade, and the city's finest viewpoints (p148) cost nothing more than a bit of effort.

Admission to most of Edinburgh's top cultural attractions, including the National Museum of Scotland (p17), the National Gallery of Scotland and many other art galleries (p21), is free, and in the evenings, for the price of a drink, you can enjoy live music for free at venues such as Sandy Bell's (p63), Jazz Bar (p62) and Whistle Binkie's (p63). For useful listings, see www.theoracle.co.uk.

>1	Old Town	36
>2	Holyrood & Arthur's Seat	64
>3	New Town	72
>4	West End & Stockbridge	96
>5	South Edinburgh	108
>6	Leith & the Waterfront	126

Shops line the streets of the Grassmarket district in the Old Town (p36)

NEIGHBOURHOODS

Modern Edinburgh sprawls over an area of 100 sq miles (259 sq km), from the shores of the Firth of Forth in the north, to the foothills of the Pentlands in the south. Fortunately, most places of interest are concentrated within the city centre.

The Old Town's maze of narrow wynds and cobbled streets, strung out along the length of the Royal Mile, is home to the city's main historical sights, as well as souvenir shops, traditional pubs and atmospheric restaurants. The Holyrood district, at the foot of the Royal Mile, contains the Scottish Parliament and the Palace of Holyroodhouse, and is the gateway to the craggy parkland of Arthur's Seat.

The New Town lies to the north of the old, on a ridge running parallel to the Royal Mile and separated from it by the valley of the Princes Street Gardens. Its regular grid of elegant Georgian terraces is a complete contrast to the chaotic tangle that characterises the Old Town, and is where you'll find most of the city's designer boutiques, wine bars and cocktail lounges.

The West End is an extension of the New Town, all Georgian elegance and upmarket shops, with the shiny new financial district called the Exchange to its south. North of the West End is Stockbridge, a trendy district with its own distinct identity, some interesting shops and a good choice of pubs and restaurants.

South Edinburgh is a catch-all neighbourhood, stretching south from the Old Town to the Pentland Hills, and taking in Tollcross, Dalry, Marchmont and Newington. Mostly it's a peaceful residential area of Victorian tenement flats and spacious garden villas. There's not much to see in the way of tourist attractions here, but there are many good restaurants, pubs and places to stay.

Edinburgh's waterfront stretches along the shore of the Firth of Forth, taking in the pretty riverside village of Cramond, the former fishing village of Newhaven and the redeveloped industrial docklands of Leith.

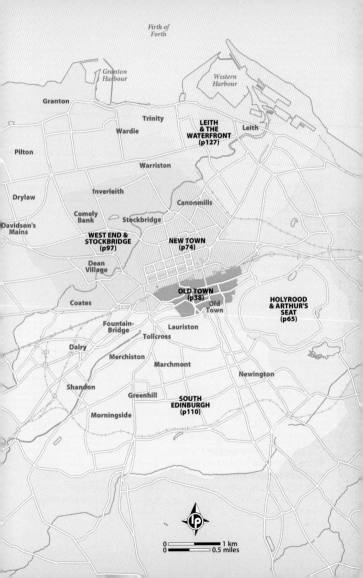

>OLD TOWN

Edinburgh's Old Town stretches along a ridge between the castle and Holyrood, and tumbles down to Grassmarket and Greyfriars Kirkyard. It's a jagged, jumbled maze of masonry riddled with closes, wynds (narrow alleys), stairs and vaults leading off the cobbled ravine of the Royal Mile. Now renovated and restored, the Old Town tenements from the 16th and 17th centuries support a thriving city-centre community, but today the street level is crammed with cafes, restaurants, bars and shops. Few visitors wander beyond the main drag of the Royal Mile, but it's worth taking time to explore the closes and wynds that lead off the street into quiet courtyards.

SEE

CANONGATE KIRK
☎ 226 5138; Canongate; admission free; ☾ 9am-6pm; 🚌 35
The kirkyard of this 17th-century church contains the graves of several famous characters, including economist and author of *The Wealth of Nations*, Adam Smith (1723–90), Agnes MacLehose (the 'Clarinda' of Robert Burns' love poems), and the 18th-century poet Robert Fergusson (1750–74). Robert Burns, a fan of Fergusson, paid for his gravestone and penned the epitaph.

CANONGATE TOLBOOTH
☎ 529 4057; 163 Canongate; admission free; ☾ 10am-5pm Mon-Sat year-round, plus 2-5pm Sun during the Edinburgh Festival; 🚌 35
Built in 1591, the picturesque Tolbooth served successively as a collection point for tolls (taxes), a council house, a courtroom and a jail. It now houses a fascinating museum, the People's Story, recording the life, work and pastimes of ordinary Edinburgh folk from the 18th century to the present day.

CITY ART CENTRE
☎ 529 3993; 2 Market St; admission free, except for temporary exhibitions; ☾ 10am-5pm Mon-Sat year-round, noon-5pm Sun Aug; 🚌 36
The largest and most populist of Edinburgh's smaller galleries, the CAC is home to the city's collection of Scottish art, ranging from the 17th to the 20th century, including works by the Scottish Colourists, as well as many fine paintings, engravings and photographs showing views of Edinburgh at various stages of its history.

CITY CHAMBERS
High St; ☾ not open to the public; 🚌 2, 23, 27, 41, 42 or 45
The imposing Georgian City Chambers were originally built by

OLD TOWN

👁 SEE

Canongate Kirk 1 H2
Canongate Tolbooth 2 H2
City Art Centre 3 E3
City Chambers 4 E3
Collective Gallery 5 E3
Dunbar's Close Garden ..6 H2
Edinburgh Castle 7 A4
Edinburgh Dungeon 8 E3
Flodden Wall 9 C5
Fruitmarket Gallery 10 E2
George Heriot's
  School 11 C5
Gladstone's Land 12 D3
Greyfriars Bobby 13 D5
Greyfriars Kirk 14 D5
Greyfriars Kirkyard 15 D5
Heart of Midlothian 16 D3
Highland Tolbooth Kirk 17 C4
Hub ....(see 17)
John Knox House 18 F3
Museum of
  Childhood 19 F3
Museum of
  Edinburgh 20 H3
Museum on the
  Mound 21 D3
National Museum of
  Scotland 22 E5
National War Museum of
  Scotland 23 A4
Old College 24 E4
Outlook Tower &
  Camera Obscura 25 C4
Parliament Hall 26 D4
Real Mary King's Close ..27 E3
Scotch Whisky
  Experience 28 C4
St Giles Cathedral 29 D3
Stills Gallery 30 E3
Talbot Rice Gallery 31 E5
Tron Kirk 32 E3
Writers' Museum 33 D3

🏠 SHOP

Aha Ha Ha 34 C4
Armstrong's 35 C4
Avalanche Records 2 ....36 E3
Bill Baber 37 C4
Blackwell's
  Bookshop 38 F4
Carson Clark Gallery 39 G3
Cookie ....(see 52)
Corniche 40 F3
Designs on
  Cashmere 41 F3
Forbidden Planet 42 F3
Fudge House of
  Edinburgh 43 G3
Geoffrey (Tailor) Inc 44 F3
Godiva 45 B5
Ian Mellis 46 C4
Joyce Forsyth
  Designer Knitwear 47 D5
Kinross Cashmere 48 D3
Liberation 49 E3
Mr Wood's Fossils 50 D4
Palenque 51 F3
Route One 52 E3
Royal Mile Whiskies 53 D3
Underground
  Solush'n 54 D3
Whiplash Trash 55 E3

🍽 EAT

Always Sunday 56 E3
Amber ....(see 28)
Black Bo's 57 F4
Café Hub ....(see 17)
Café Marlayne 58 E4
David Bann 59 G4
Doric Tavern 60 D3
Forest Café 61 E5
Fruitmarket Gallery
  Cafe ....(see 10)
Gordon's Trattoria 62 E3

Grain Store 63 D4
Maison Bleue 64 C4
Maxie's Bistro 65 C4
Mum's 66 D5
North Bridge
  Brasserie 67 E3
Ondine 68 D4
Pancho Villa's 69 G3
Petit Paris 70 C4
Tower 71 D5
Witchery by
  the Castle 72 C4

🍷 DRINK

Assembly Bar 73 E5
Beehive Inn 74 C5
Bow Bar 75 C4
Ecco Vino 76 D3
Jolly Judge 77 D3
Malt Shovel 78 E3
Royal Mile Tavern 79 F3
Villager 80 D4
White Hart Inn 81 C4

⭐ PLAY

Bedlam Theatre 82 D5
Bongo Club 83 H3
Cabaret Voltaire 84 E4
Caves 85 F4
Dance Base 86 C5
Jazz Bar 87 F4
Liquid Room 88 D4
Opium 89 D4
Pleasance
  Cabaret Bar 90 G4
Red Vodka Club 91 D4
Royal Oak 92 F4
Sandy Bell's 93 D5
Studio 24 ....94 H2
Whistle Binkie's 95 F3

Please see over for map

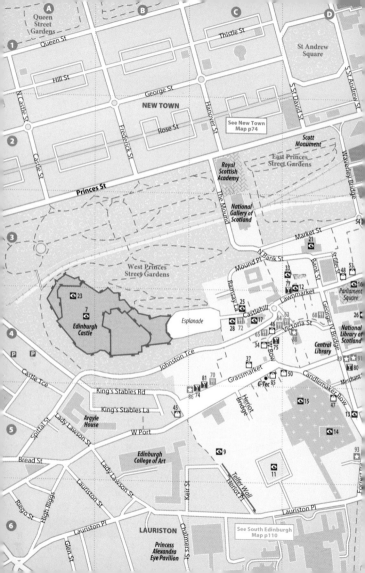

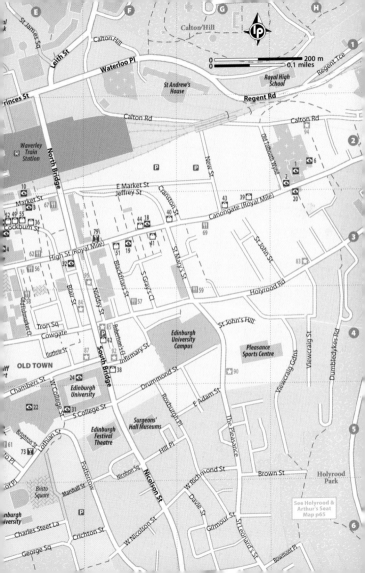

John Adam (brother of Robert) between 1753 and 1761 to serve as the Royal Exchange – a covered meeting place for city merchants – replacing the traditional meeting place of the Mercat Cross. However, the merchants preferred their old stamping ground in the street and the building has housed the offices of the city council since 1811. Though only four storeys high on the Royal Mile side, the building plummets 12 storeys on the northern side, overlooking Cockburn St.

COLLECTIVE GALLERY

☎ 220 1260; www.collectivegallery .net; 22-28 Cockburn St; admission free; 🕘 11am-5pm Tue-Sun; 🚌 all North Bridge buses

The Collective is an artist-run gallery with regularly changing exhibitions by contemporary artists, both Scottish and international.

DUNBAR'S CLOSE GARDEN

Canongate; admission free; 🕘 24hr; 🚌 35

Tucked away at the end of an Old Town close, this walled garden has been laid out in the style of the 17th century, with gravel paths, neatly trimmed shrubs, herbs and flowers and mature trees. A hidden gem, and an oasis of tranquillity amid the bustle of the Royal Mile.

EDINBURGH CASTLE

☎ 225 9846; Castlehill; adult/child/concession incl audio guide £14/7.50/11.20; 🕘 9.30am-6pm Apr-Sep, 9.30am-5pm Oct-Mar, 11am-5pm 1 & 2 Jan, closed 25 & 26 Dec, last ticket sold 45min before closing; 🚌 2, 23, 27, 41, 42 or 45

Edinburgh Castle is Scotland's most popular pay-to-enter tourist attraction, pulling in over a million visitors each year. To avoid the crowds, try to visit early or late

THE STONE OF DESTINY

At the coronation ceremony of almost every English, and later British, monarch from Edward II in 1307 to Elizabeth II in 1953, the king- or queen-to-be sat on a throne that housed the legendary Stone of Destiny. The stone – said to have originated in the Holy Land, and on which Scottish kings placed their feet (not their bums; the English got that bit wrong) during their coronation – was stolen from Scone Abbey near Perth by King Edward I of England in 1296. It was taken to London's Westminster Abbey and there it remained for seven centuries, an enduring symbol of Scotland's subjugation by England.

The stone was returned to Scotland in 1996 in a failed attempt to boost the flagging popularity of the Conservative Party prior to a general election – the Scots said thanks very much for the stone and then, in May 1997, voted every Conservative MP in Scotland into oblivion.

in the day. The castle has played a pivotal role in Scottish history, both as a royal residence and as a military stronghold, and dominates the city centre from its lofty crag. The best views of the fortress are from the Vennel, south of the Grassmarket, and from the summit of Calton Hill (p73). For more info on visiting the castle see p12.

🇨 EDINBURGH DUNGEON
☎ 240 1000; 31 Market St; adult/child £15.50/11.50; ⏱ 10am-7pm Jul & Aug, 10am-5pm Apr-Jun, Sep & Oct, 11am-4pm Mon-Fri & 10.30am-4.30pm Sat & Sun Nov-Mar; 🚌 36; ♿

This manufactured attraction combines gruesome tableaux of torture and degradation with live actors who perform scary little sketches along the way. There's also a 'horror labyrinth', a creepy mirror maze inhabited by the ghost of a little drummer boy. Mildly amusing in a large group, mildly embarrassing in a small one and genuinely terrifying for small children. Children under 15 must be accompanied by an adult; not recommended for kids under eight.

🇨 FLODDEN WALL
🚌 2, 23, 27 or 45

At the western end of the Grassmarket a narrow close called the Vennel leads steeply up to one of the few surviving fragments of the city wall that was built in the early 16th century as protection against a feared English invasion. Beyond it is the Telfer Wall, a later extension that continues to Lauriston Pl.

🇨 FRUITMARKET GALLERY
☎ 225 2383; www.fruitmarket.co.uk; 45 Market St; admission free; ⏱ 11am-6pm Mon-Sat, noon-5pm Sun; 🚌 36; ♿

One of the city's most innovative galleries, the Fruitmarket showcases contemporary Scottish and international artists; it also has an excellent arts bookshop and cafe (p53). There are around half a dozen exhibitions a year, ranging from paintings to installations to light-based artworks.

🇨 GEORGE HERIOT'S SCHOOL
☎ 229 7263; Lauriston Pl; ⏱ Sep only; 🚌 23 or 27

One of the most impressive buildings in the Old Town, this school was built in the 17th century with funds bequeathed by George Heriot (goldsmith and banker to King James VI, and popularly known as Jinglin' Geordie). It was originally a school and home for orphaned children, but became a fee-paying public school in 1886. It's open to the public on Doors Open Day (www.doorsopendays .org.uk) in September.

🟢 GLADSTONE'S LAND

☎ 226 5856; 477 Lawnmarket; adult/
child £5.50/4.50; ⏱ 10am-6.30pm Jul &
Aug, 10am-5pm Apr-Jun, Sep & Oct; 🚌 2,
23, 27, 41, 42 or 45

In 1617 Thomas Gledstanes, a
17th-century merchant (and an-
cestor of the 19th-century British
prime minister William Gladstone)
bought this tenement building,
which gives a fascinating glimpse
of the Old Town's past. The
comfortable interior contains fine
painted ceilings, walls and beams
and some splendid furniture from
the 17th and 18th centuries. The
volunteer guides provide a wealth
of anecdotes.

🟢 GREYFRIARS BOBBY

cnr George IV Bridge & Candlemaker
Row; 🚌 2, 23, 27, 41, 42 or 45

One of Edinburgh's most popular
memorials is the tiny statue of
Greyfriars Bobby, a Skye terrier
who maintained a vigil over the
grave of his master, an Edinburgh
police officer, from 1858 to 1872.
The story was immortalised (and
romanticised) by Eleanor Atkinson
in her 1912 novel *Greyfriars Bobby*,
which was made into a movie in
1961 by – who else? – Walt Disney
(a remake was released in 2005).
Bobby's grave – marked by a
small, pink granite stone – is just
inside the entrance to Greyfriars

Greyfriars Bobby is still waiting outside the Greyfriars Kirkyard

Kirkyard (below). His original collar and bowl are in the Museum of Edinburgh (p44).

◎ GREYFRIARS KIRK & KIRKYARD

☎ 226 5429; www.greyfriarskirk.com; Candlemaker Row; admission free; ⏱ 10.30am-4.30pm Mon-Fri & 10.30am-2.30pm Sat Apr-Oct, 1.30-3.30pm Thu Nov-Mar; 🚌 2, 23, 27, 41, 42 or 45; ♿

The church of Greyfriars is famous as the spot where the National Covenant was signed in 1638, rejecting Charles I's attempts to impose episcopacy and affirming the independence of the Scottish Church. Many who signed it were later executed in the Grassmarket and, in 1679, 1200 Covenanters were held prisoner in terrible conditions in an enclosure in the far corner of the kirkyard.

Inside the church is a small exhibition on the National Covenant, and an original portrait of Greyfriars Bobby (opposite) dating from 1867. At 12.30pm on Sundays there are church services in Gaelic.

The Kirkyard is one of Edinburgh's spookiest spots. Many famous Edinburgh names are buried here, including poet Allan Ramsay (1686–1758), architect William Adam (1689–1748), and William Smellie (1740–95), editor of the first edition of Encyclopaedia Britannica. In the southwest corner is the Covenanters' Prison,

a series of enclosed tombs reputedly haunted by a poltergeist (see p16).

◎ HEART OF MIDLOTHIAN

High St; 🚌 2, 23, 27, 41, 42 or 45

Outside the western door of St Giles Cathedral is a cobblestone heart set into the paving that marks the site of the 15th-century Tolbooth. The Tolbooth served variously as a meeting place for parliament and the town council before becoming law courts and, finally, a notorious prison and place of execution. Immortalised in Sir Walter Scott's novel *The Heart of Midlothian,* the Tolbooth was demolished in the 19th century. Passers-by traditionally spit on the heart for good luck (don't stand downwind!).

◎ HIGHLAND TOLBOOTH KIRK

Castlehill; 🚌 2, 23, 27, 41, 42 or 45; ♿

Edinburgh's tallest spire (71.7m) was built in the 1840s by James Graham and Augustus Pugin (architect of London's Houses of Parliament) and takes its name from Gaelic services held here in the 19th century for Edinburgh's Highland congregations. The refurbished interior houses the **Hub** (☎ 473 2015; www.thehub-edinburgh.com; admission free; ⏱ ticket centre 10am-5pm Mon-Sat), the ticket office and information centre for the Edinburgh Festival and other events.

☑ JOHN KNOX HOUSE

☎ 556 9579; 43-45 High St; adult/child £4/1; ⏱ 10am-6pm Mon-Sat year-round, noon-6pm Sun Jul & Aug; 🚌 35

Edinburgh's oldest surviving tenement, dating from around 1490, has an outside staircase, overhanging upper floors and crowstepped gables; Calvinist firebrand John Knox is thought to have lived here from 1561 to 1572. The labyrinthine interior has some beautiful painted timber ceilings and interesting displays on Knox's life and work.

☑ MUSEUM OF CHILDHOOD

☎ 529 4142; 42 High St; admission free; ⏱ 10am-5pm Mon-Sat, noon-5pm Sun; 🚌 35

Known as 'the noisiest museum in the world' (it's often overrun with screaming kids), this place covers serious issues related to child-hood – health, education, upbringing and so on. It also has an enormous collection of toys, games and books: everything from Victorian dolls to a video history of the 1960s Gerry Anderson TV puppet series, *Thunderbirds*.

☑ MUSEUM OF EDINBURGH

☎ 529 4143; 142 Canongate; admission free; ⏱ 10am-5pm Mon-Sat year-round, noon-5pm Sun Aug; 🚌 35

The labyrinth of oak-panelled rooms and creaky wooden floors

that is Huntly House (built 1570) is home to a lot of less-than-riveting displays, but there are some gems worth seeking out – an original copy of the National Covenant signed in Greyfriars Kirkyard in 1638, an interesting exhibit on the history of the One O'Clock Gun (p78), and the dog collar and feeding bowl that belonged to Greyfriars Bobby (p42).

☑ MUSEUM ON THE MOUND

☎ 243 5464; The Mound; admission free; ⏱ 10am-5pm Tue-Fri, 1-5pm Sat & Sun; 🚌 2, 23, 27, 41, 42 or 45

Housed in the Bank of Scotland's splendid Georgian HQ, this little museum is a treasure trove of gold coins, bullion chests, safes, banknotes, forgeries, cartoons and lots of fascinating old documents and photographs charting the history of Scotland's oldest bank.

☑ NATIONAL MUSEUM OF SCOTLAND

☎ 247 4422; www.nms.ac.uk; Chambers St; admission free, fee for special exhibitions; ⏱ 10am-5pm, closed 25 Dec; 🚌 2, 23, 27, 35, 41, 42 or 45; ♿

Consisting of two buildings (the 19th-century Royal Museum and the late-20th-century Museum of Scotland) which have been cleverly joined together, the National Museum of Scotland covers culture, science, art and nature, from

Time for tea at the National Museum of Scotland (p44)

ancient fossils to Formula 1 racing cars. Audioguides are available in several languages, and volunteers give free 45-minute guided tours. For more details, see p17.

NATIONAL WAR MUSEUM OF SCOTLAND

☎ 225 7534; Edinburgh Castle, Castle-hill; admission incl in Edinburgh Castle ticket; ⏱ 9.45am-5.45pm Apr-Oct, 9.45am-4.45pm Nov-Mar; 🚌 2, 23, 27, 41, 42 or 45; ♿

Exhibits concentrate on individual stories of courage, determination and heartbreak rather than broad historical narratives, and include unusual items such as a varnished set of elephant's toenails and the story of Bob the Dog, regimental mascot of the 1st Battalion Scots Fusilier Guards, who chased cannonballs at the Battle of Inkerman and was awarded his own medal.

OLD COLLEGE

South Bridge; 🚌 all South Bridge buses

Edinburgh University's Old College is a neoclassical masterpiece designed by Robert Adam in 1789; today it is home to the univeristy's law faculty. At the far end of the quad you'll find the Talbot Rice Gallery (p47).

OUTLOOK TOWER & CAMERA OBSCURA

☎ 226 3709; Castlehill; adult/child £9.25/6.25; ⏱ 9.30am-7.30pm Jul & Aug, 9.30am-6pm Apr-Jun, Sep & Oct, 10am-5pm Nov-Mar; 🚌 2, 23, 27, 41, 42 or 45

An entertaining commentary accompanies this Heath Robinson–ish 19th-century device that uses lenses and mirrors to throw a live image of the city onto a large horizontal screen. Stairs lead up through various displays on optics to the Outlook Tower, which offers great views over the city.

PARLIAMENT HALL

☎ 348 5355; 11 Parliament Sq; admission free; ⏱ 10am-4pm Mon-Fri; 🚌 2, 23, 27, 41, 42 or 45

This magnificent 17th-century hall, with original oak hammer-beam roof, is where the original Scottish Parliament met before its dissolution in 1707. Now used by lawyers and their clients as a meeting place, it's open to the public. As you enter (there's a sign outside saying 'Parliament Hall; Court of Session') you'll see the reception desk in front of you; the hall is through the double doors immediately on your right.

REAL MARY KING'S CLOSE

☎ 0870 243 0160; 2 Warriston's Close, High St; adult/child £11/6; ⏱ 10am-9pm Apr-Oct, to 11pm Aug, 10am-5pm Sun-Thu & 10am-9pm Fri & Sat Nov-Mar; 🚌 2, 23, 27, 41, 42 or 45

This medieval Old Town alley has survived almost unchanged for 250 years amid the foundations of the City Chambers, a spooky, subterranean labyrinth that gives an insight into life in 17th-century Edinburgh. The guided tour can seem a little naff, milking the scary and scatological aspects of the close's history for all they're worth, but something about the crumbling 17th-century tenement rooms and the ancient smell of stone and dust makes the hairs rise on the back of your neck. Then there's wee Annie's room,

where a psychic claimed to have been approached by the ghost of a little girl. It's hard to tell what's more spooky, the story of the ghostly girl or the bizarre heap of dolls and teddies left in a corner by sympathetic visitors.

SCOTCH WHISKY EXPERIENCE

☎ 220 0441; 354 Castlehill; adult/child incl tour & tasting £11.50/5.95; ⏱ 10am-6.30pm Jun-Aug, 10am-6pm Sep-May; 🚌 2, 23, 27, 41, 42 or 45; ♿ 📶

Johnnie Walker meets Walt Disney in this series of interactive exhibits telling the story of whisky from barley to bottle. The tour kicks off with a wee taste of the real thing (soft drinks for the under-18s), and involves a 'whisky-barrel ride' (mildly embarrassing for anyone over 12) through 'smell-surround' tableaux depicting the history of the national drink, before finishing in a shop full of whisky. The onsite restaurant Amber (p52) is recommended.

ST GILES CATHEDRAL

☎ 225 9442; www.stgilescathedral.org.uk; High St; admission free, £3 donation suggested; ⏱ 9am-7pm Mon-Fri, 9am-5pm Sat & 1-5pm Sun May-Sep, 9am-5pm Mon-Sat & 1-5pm Sun Oct-Apr; 🚌 2, 23, 27, 41 or 45

The great grey bulk of St Giles Cathedral, capped by a beautiful

MARY KING'S CLOSE

Legend has it that during a plague in 1645 the disease-ridden inhabitants of Mary King's Close (an alley on the northern side of the Royal Mile) were walled up in their houses and left to perish. When the lifeless bodies were eventually cleared from the houses, they were so stiff that workmen had to hack off limbs to get them through the small doorways and narrow, twisting stairs. From that day on, the close was said to be haunted by the spirits of the plague victims. When the Royal Exchange (now the City Chambers) was constructed between 1753 and 1761, it was built over the lower levels of Mary King's Close, which were left intact beneath the building. Abandoned for 250 years, this spooky subterranean world is now open to the public (see Real Mary King's Close, opposite).

15th-century crown spire, dominates the Royal Mile. John Knox served as minister here, preaching his uncompromising Calvinist message, but its proudest moment came in 1637 when a woman called Jenny Geddes, incensed at the king's attempts to impose bishops on Scotland, hurled her stool at the dean and ignited a riot whose aftermath led to the signing of the National Covenant at Greyfriars the following year. A plaque marks the spot where Geddes launched her protest.

One of the most interesting corners of the church is the Thistle Chapel, built between 1909 and 1911 for the Knights of the Most Ancient and Most Noble Order of the Thistle. The elaborately carved Gothic-style stalls have canopies topped with the helms and arms of the 16 knights – look out for the bagpipe-playing angel amid the vaulting.

◙ STILLS GALLERY
☎ 622 6200; www.stills.org; 23 Cockburn St; admission free; ⏰ 11am-9pm Mon-Thu, to 6pm Fri-Sun; 🚌 36; ♿
Scotland's top photographic gallery hosts changing exhibitions of the best of international contemporary photography.

◙ TALBOT RICE GALLERY
☎ 650 2210; www.trg.ed.ac.uk; Old College, South Bridge; admission free; ⏰ 10am-5pm Tue-Sat, daily during Edinburgh Festival; 🚌 all South Bridge buses
This small art gallery has two exhibition spaces. The neoclassical Georgian Gallery, designed by William Playfair, houses a permanent collection of works by old masters, including Dutch landscapes by Van de Velde and Van der Meulen, and a striking bronze anatomical figure of a horse, created in Florence in 1598.

The White Gallery, a more modern space, is used to exhibit the works of contemporary Scottish painters and sculptors.

◎ TRON KIRK
☎ 225 8408; cnr High St & South Bridge; admission free; ◷ 10am-5.30pm Apr-Oct, noon-5pm Nov-Mar; 🚌 all South Bridge buses

Built in 1637, and taking its name from the *tron*, or public weigh-bridge, that once stood on the site, this church is famous for its magnificent oak hammer-beam roof, which rivals that in the Great Hall at Edinburgh Castle (p12). The floor has been excavated by archaeologists to reveal the cobbled surface of Marlin's Wynd, a late-16th-century alley with the remains of cellars, staircases and medieval drains on either side.

◎ WRITERS' MUSEUM
☎ 529 4901; Lady Stair's Close, Lawnmarket; admission free; ◷ 10am-5pm Mon-Sat year-round, 2-5pm Sun Aug; 🚌 2, 23, 27, 41, 42 or 45

Lady Stair's House, originally built in 1622 and restored in grand Jacobean style, houses a fascinating museum dedicated to Robert Burns, Sir Walter Scott and Robert Louis Stevenson. In the basement is a tall mahogany cabinet built by none other than the notorious Deacon Brodie. It

sat in Stevenson's bedroom when he was a child, and played a part in the author's inspiration for his novel *The Strange Tale of Dr Jekyll and Mr Hyde*.

🛍 SHOP

▢ AHA HA HA *Toys & Gifts*
☎ 220 5252; 99 West Bow; ◷ noon-5pm Sun Aug & Dec; 🚌 2

The guys at Aha Ha Ha have enough plastic poo, fake vomit, stink bombs and remote-control electronic farting machines to keep your average Dennis the Menace happy for a month or more. It's also a good place to go if you're looking for Halloween masks, costumes, magic tricks and practical jokes.

▢ ARMSTRONG'S *Fashion*
☎ 220 5557; www.armstrongsvintage.co.uk; 83 Grassmarket; ◷ 10am-5.30pm Mon-Thu, 10am-6pm Fri & Sat, noon-6pm Sun; 🚌 2

Armstrong's is an Edinburgh fashion institution (established in 1840, no less), a quality vintage clothes emporium offering everything from elegant 1940s dresses to funky 1970s flares. As well as having retro fashion, it's a great place to hunt for 'previously owned' kilts and Harris tweed, or to seek inspiration for that fancy-dress party.

Getting frocked up at Armstrong's (p48)

☎ AVALANCHE RECORDS *Music*
☎ 225 3939; 63 Cockburn St;
🕑 9.30am-6pm Mon-Sat, noon-6pm
Sun; 🚌 all South Bridge buses
Along with Fopp (p79), Avalanche
is a sacred place of pilgrimage for
music fans in search of good-value
CDs, especially indie, rock and
punk.

☐ BILL BABER *Fashion*
☎ 225 3249; www.billbaber.com;
66 Grassmarket; 🕑 9am-5.30pm
Mon-Sat; 🚌 2
This family run designer knitwear
studio has been in the business
for more than 30 years, produc-

ing stylish and colourful creations
using linen, merino wool, silk and
cotton.

☐ BLACKWELL'S BOOKSHOP
Books
☎ 622 8222; www.blackwell.co.uk;
53-62 South Bridge; 🕑 9am-8pm Mon
& Wed-Sat, 9.30am-8pm Tue, noon-6pm
Sun; 🚌 all South Bridge buses
Blackwell's four floors have an
admirable selection of reading
matter, with an excellent range of
academic, foreign language and
Scottish history titles.

☐ CARSON CLARK GALLERY
Antiques & Maps
☎ 556 4710; 181-183 Canongate;
🕑 10.30am-5.30pm Mon-Sat; 🚌 35
Scotland's leading map specialist
has knowledgeable staff who are
more than happy to advise on
their interesting range of original
and facsimile antique maps,
charts and plans of Scotland,
Europe and the rest of the world.
The shop also has on offer some
gorgeous antique globes.

☐ CORNICHE *Fashion*
☎ 556 3707; www.corniche.org.uk; 2
Jeffrey St; 🕑 10.30am-5.30pm Mon-
Sat; 🚌 35
A major stockist of designer
clothes for women, with a
selection of big-name labels such
as Jean-Paul Gaultier, Vivienne

COCKBURN STREET

Cockburn St, curving down from the Royal Mile to Waverley train station, is the beating heart of Edinburgh's teenage shopping scene, lined with quirky independent stores selling everything from Goth gear and body piercings to incense and healing crystals. Here you'll find the city's best record shops, Underground Solush'n (p52) and Avalanche (p49), as well as:

Cookie (☎ 622 7260; 29 Cockburn St) Cute party dresses.
Liberation (☎ 225 9831; 45 Cockburn St) T-shirts with slogans.
Route One (☎ 226 2131; www.routeone.co.uk; 29 Cockburn St) Skate and BMX gear.
Whiplash Trash (☎ 226 1005; 53 Cockburn St) Tattoos and body piercings.

Westwood, Anna Sui, Katharine Hamnett and Alexander McQueen. The branch next door concentrates on designer menswear.

🏠 DESIGNS ON CASHMERE
Fashion
☎ 556 6394; www.designsoncashmere.com; 28 High St; 🕙 10am-5.30pm Mon-Sat; 🚌 all South Bridge buses
Designs on Cashmere is a good place to shop for top-quality cashmere clothing for both men and women, along with cashmere scarves, hats, gloves, snoods and capes.

🏠 FORBIDDEN PLANET *Fashion*
☎ 225 8613; www.forbiddenplanet.co.uk; 40-41 South Bridge; 🕙 10am-5.30pm Mon-Wed, Fri & Sat, 10am-6pm Thu, noon-5pm Sun; 🚌 all South Bridge buses
This place stocks a wide range of sci-fi comics, graphic novels, DVDs and T-shirts, as well as *Star Trek*, *Simpsons* and *South Park*

merchandise. It's also the place for *Alien vs Predator* action figures, Bleeding Edge dolls and Kurt Cobain lunchboxes (if you have to ask, you don't wanna know…).

🏠 FUDGE HOUSE OF EDINBURGH *Food & Drink*
☎ 556 4172; www.fudgehouse.co.uk; 197 Canongate; 🕙 10am-5.30pm; 🚌 35
A monument to the Scots' sweet tooth, this family business offers acres of homemade fudge, including chocolate and peppermint, rum and raisin, hazelnut, and tasty Highland cream. Mmmmm. There's a coffee shop too.

🏠 GEOFFREY (TAILOR) INC
Fashion
☎ 557 0256; www.geoffreykilts.co.uk; 57-61 High St; 🕙 9am-5.30pm Mon-Wed, Fri & Sat, 9am-7pm Thu, 10am-5pm Sun; 🚌 all South Bridge buses
Geoffrey can fit you out in traditional Highland dress, run

up a kilt in your own clan tartan, or just hire out the gear for a wedding or other special event. Its on-site offshoot, **21st Century Kilts** (www.21stcenturykilts.co.uk), offers modern fashion kilts in a variety of fabrics; celebrity customers include Robbie Williams and Vin Diesel.

GODIVA *Fashion*
☎ 221 9212; www.godivaboutique. co.uk; 9 West Port; ⏰ 10.30am-6.30pm Mon-Fri, to 6pm Sat, noon-5pm Sun; 🚌 2
This unconventional and innovative boutique specialising in both vintage and modern cutting-edge designs won Best New Designer prize in the Scottish Variety Awards 2010.

IAN MELLIS *Food & Drink*
☎ 226 6215; www.mellischeese.co.uk; 30a Victoria St; ⏰ 10am-6pm Mon-Fri, 9.30am-6pm Sat; 🚌 2, 23, 27, 41 or 42
Scotland's finest cheesemonger purveys the best of British and Irish cheeses. This is the place to purchase traditional Scottish cheeses, from smooth Lanark Blue (the Scottish Roquefort) to sharp Isle of Mull Cheddar. There's also a branch in Stockbridge (p101).

JOYCE FORSYTH DESIGNER KNITWEAR *Fashion*
☎ 220 4112; 42 Candlemaker Row; ⏰ 10am-5.30pm Tue-Sat; 🚌 2, 23, 27, 41 or 42

The colourful knitwear at this intriguing little shop will drag your ideas about woollens firmly into the 21st century. Ms Forsyth's trademark design is a flamboyant flared woollen coat (can be knitted to order in colours of your own choice), but there are also jackets, jumpers, hats, scarves and shawls.

KINROSS CASHMERE *Fashion*
☎ 226 1577; www.cashmerestore.com; 2 St Giles St; ⏰ 10am-6pm Mon-Sat, 11am-4.30pm Sun; 🚌 2, 23, 27, 41 or 42
This shop stocks a wide range of traditional and modern knitwear in more than 30 colours, plus a big choice of cashmere accessories such as scarves and shawls.

MR WOOD'S FOSSILS *Toys & Gifts*
☎ 220 1344; 5 Cowgatehead; ⏰ 10am-5.30pm Mon-Sat; 🚌 2
Founded by the famous fossil hunter who discovered 'Lizzie', the oldest fossil reptile yet discovered, this fascinating speciality shop has a wide range of minerals, gems, fossils and other geological gifts.

PALENQUE *Jewellery*
☎ 557 9553; www.palenquejewellery .co.uk; 56 High St; ⏰ 10am-5.30pm Mon-Sat; 🚌 all South Bridge buses
Palenque is a treasure trove of contemporary silver jewellery and handcrafted accessories made

OLD TOWN > EAT

using ceramics, textiles and metal-work. There's a second branch in the New Town (p81).

ROYAL MILE WHISKIES
Food & Drink
☎ 225 3383; www.royalmilewhiskies.co.uk; 379 High St; ⏰ 10am-6pm Mon-Sat, 12.30-6pm Sun, to 8pm daily Jul–mid-Sep; 🚍 2, 23, 27, 41 or 42
If it's a drop of the cratur ye're after, this place has a selection of single malts in miniature and full-size bottles. There's also a range of blended whiskies, Irish whiskey and bourbon, and you can buy online too.

UNDERGROUND SOLUSH'N
Music
☎ 226 2242; 9 Cockburn St; ⏰ 10am-6pm Mon-Wed, Fri & Sat, 10am-7pm Thu, noon-6pm Sun; 🚍 all South Bridge buses
A paradise for searchers of new and secondhand vinyl, this place has thousands of records – techno, house, jungle, hip-hop, R&B, funk, soul and 45s – plus a (smaller) selection of CDs, T-shirts, videos, books and merchandise. It's also a good place to find out what's happening on the local music/clubbing scene.

EAT

ALWAYS SUNDAY *Cafe* £
☎ 622 0667; 170 High St; ⏰ 8am-6pm Mon-Fri, 9am-6pm Sat & Sun; 🚍 2, 23, 27, 41 or 42

If the mere thought of a greasy fry-up is enough to put you off your breakfast, head instead for this bright and breezy cafe which dishes up hearty but healthy grub such as fresh fruit smoothies, crisp salads, homemade soups and speciality sandwiches, all washed down with Fairtrade coffee or herbal tea.

AMBER *Scottish* ££
☎ 477 8477; www.amber-restaurant.co.uk; 354 Castlehill; ⏰ noon-3.45pm daily & 7-9pm Tue-Sat; 🚍 2, 23, 27, 41, 42 or 45
You simply have to love a place where the waiter greets you with the words 'My name is Craig, and I'll be your whisky adviser for this evening'. Located in the Scotch Whisky Heritage Centre (p46), this romantic restaurant manages to avoid tourist clichés and creates genuinely interesting dishes using the best of Scottish produce.

BLACK BO'S *Vegetarian* ££
☎ 557 6136; 57-61 Blackfriars St; ⏰ 6-10pm daily; 🚍 35; Ⓥ
You can't accuse the chef at Black Bo's, a very popular vegetarian and vegan eatery located just off the Royal Mile, of being unadventurous. Check the daily specials, which are always interesting – beetroot and cashew balls stuffed with feta cheese, for example.

🍴 CAFÉ HUB *Bistro* ££
☎ 473 2067; Castlehill; ⏲ 9.30am-10pm daily; 🚌 2, 23, 27, 41, 42 or 45
A Gothic hall beneath the Highland Tolbooth Kirk (p43) – now home to the Edinburgh Festival offices – has been transformed into this bright and breezy bistro with zingy yellow walls, cobalt-blue furniture and lots of imagination. Drop in for cake and cappuccino, or try something more filling – fish chowder with crusty bread, or vegetable chilli with corn chips and rice.

🍴 CAFÉ MARLAYNE
French ££
☎ 225 3838; 7 Old Fishmarket Close, High St; ⏲ noon-2pm & 6-10pm, closed Sun & Mon Oct-Mar; 🚌 2, 23, 27, 41 or 42
This second branch of the New Town French bistro (p83) is a hidden gem, stashed away down a steep cobbled alley off the Royal Mile. The mazelike, vaulted dining area sports beech tables and pastel-coloured chairs, with contemporary paintings on cream walls, a daily menu of fresh market produce and a lovely little outdoor terrace.

🍴 DAVID BANN
Vegetarian ££-£££
☎ 556 5888; www.davidbann.com; 56-58 St Mary's St; ⏲ noon-10pm Mon-Fri, 11am-10pm Sat & Sun; 🚌 35; Ⓥ

If you want to convince a carnivorous friend that cuisine à la veg can be every bit as tasty and inventive as a meat-muncher's menu, take them to David Bann's stylish restaurant. Dishes such as beetroot, apple and Dunsyre blue cheese pudding, and crepe of Thai-spiced broccoli and smoked tofu, are guaranteed to win converts.

🍴 DORIC TAVERN *Scottish* ££
☎ 225 1084; 15-16 Market St; ⏲ 11am-1am; 🚌 36
One of Edinburgh's favourite eateries, this 1st-floor bistro (entrance stairs to the right of the Doric Bar) is handy for both Princes St and the Royal Mile. Wooden floors, warm ochre walls and window tables with views of the Scott Monument complement a menu of fresh Scottish produce.

🍴 FOREST CAFÉ *Cafe* £
☎ 220 4538; www.theforest.org.uk; 3 Bristo Pl; ⏲ noon-9pm; 🚌 2, 23, 27, 41 or 42; 🛜 Ⓥ
A chilled-out and comfortably scuffed-around-the-edges antidote to squeaky-clean style bars, this volunteer-run, not-for-profit art space and café serves up humongous helpings of hearty vegetarian and vegan fodder, ranging from burritos to falafel burgers.

Tucking into vegetarian delights at David Bann (p53)

🍴 FRUITMARKET GALLERY CAFE *Cafe*   £
☎ 226 1843; 45 Market St; 🕑 11am-5.30pm Mon-Sat, noon-4.30pm Sun; 🚍 35
After checking out the art in the Fruitmarket Gallery (p41), check out the menu in its stylish cafe – fresh sandwiches, big crunchy salads and hot ciabatta melts – or settle down with a cappuccino to browse the book you just bought in the adjacent art bookshop.

🍴 GORDON'S TRATTORIA
Italian   ££
☎ 225 7992; 231 High St; 🕑 noon-midnight Sun-Thu, noon-3am Fri & Sat; 🚍 all South Bridge buses

The delicious aroma of garlic bread wafting into the street will guide you into this snug haven of wisecracking waiters and hearty Italian comfort food. In summer you can chomp on pizza and slurp wine while comfortably seated at a pavement table, and late-night hours means that Gordon's often develops a bit of a party atmosphere after midnight on Friday and Saturday.

🍴 GRAIN STORE *French/Scottish*   ££
☎ 225 7635; www.grainstore-restaurant.co.uk; 30 Victoria St; 🕑 lunch & dinner; 🚍 2, 23, 27, 41 or 42

An atmospheric upstairs dining room on picturesque Victoria St, the Grain Store has a well-earned reputation for serving the finest Scottish produce, perfectly prepared – from seared scallops with peas and bacon, to tender wild hare cooked in a pastry parcel. A three-course lunch for £15 is good value.

MAISON BLEUE
International   ££
☎ 226 1900; 36-38 Victoria St; ☽ noon-3pm & 5-10pm Sun-Wed, noon-10pm Sun-Thu, noon-11pm Fri & Sat; ☒ 2, 23, 27, 41 or 42

Eating here is a comfortably laid-back affair – the candlelit ground-floor dining room has basketwork chairs, chunky wooden tables and modern art on bare stone walls; upstairs is brighter and more cafe-like. The menu lists *bouchées* (French for 'mouthfuls') – starter-size helpings of which you can have as many or as few as you wish – and the food is an eclectic mix of European, North African and Far Eastern influences.

MAXIE'S BISTRO
International   ££
☎ 226 7770; 5b Johnston Tce; ☽ 11am-11pm; ☒ 2, 23, 27, 41 or 42

This candlelit cellar bistro, with its cushion-lined nooks set amid stone walls, cream plaster and wooden beams, is a pleasant

enough setting for a cosy dinner, but at summer lunchtimes people queue for the outdoor tables on Victoria Tce, with great views over Victoria St. The dependable food – Maxie's has been in the food business for more than 20 years – ranges from pastas, steaks and stir-fries to superb seafood platters and daily specials.

MUM'S *Cafe*   £
☎ 260 9806; www.monstermashcafe.co.uk; 4a Forrest Rd; ☽ 8am-10pm Mon-Fri, 9am-10pm Sat, 10am-10pm Sun; ☒ 2, 23, 27, 41 or 42

After a change of name due to management fall-outs, the original founder of Monster Mash has reopened with a new name. This nostalgia-fuelled cafe continues to serve up classic British comfort food of the 1950s – bangers and mash, shepherd's pie, fish and chips. But there's a twist – the food is all top-quality nosh freshly prepared from local produce, including Crombie's gourmet sausages. And there's even a wine list!

NORTH BRIDGE BRASSERIE
Scottish   ££-£££
☎ 622 2900; www.northbridge-brasserie.com; 20 North Bridge; ☽ noon-2pm & 5.30-10pm daily; ☒ all North Bridge & Princes St buses

This stylish brasserie inhabits the former lobby of the *Scots-*

Steve Hall
Senior Manager at the Witchery by the Castle (p58)

As manager of one of Edinburgh's top restaurants, where would you go to enjoy a meal in your time off? As well as Rhubarb (p71) and the Tower (p57), I think the food at Ondine (p57) is consistently excellent, and the restaurant itself is lovely. At the other end of the budget spectrum, I'm a great fan of The Dogs (p88) where the atmosphere is great and the food offers absolutely outstanding value for money – you could spend more in a chip shop! I also like Escargot Bleu (p84) and Escargot Blanc (p103), very authentic French cuisine – it would be hard to find cooking that capable, at that price, in France. **And what about places to drink?** Bramble (p90) for good cocktails, and Tigerlily (p92) for style and service. And Joseph Pearce's (p91) is a great old boozer that has been nicely modernised; it's family-friendly and does decent food too.

man newspaper building (now the Scotsman Hotel), a huge airy hall with four massive marble columns. Book a table up on the balcony, where you can admire the gilded capitals or gaze down on the street from the arched windows. The menu takes its inspiration from hearty Scots fare, ranging from hot buttered crab on sourdough toast to roast rump of lamb with haggis and mashed potato.

ONDINE Seafood   £££
☎ 226 1888; www.ondinerestaurant.co.uk; 2 George IV Bridge; ⏱ noon-10pm; 🚌 2, 23, 27, 41 or 42

New on the scene in 2009, Ondine has rapidly become one of Edinburgh's finest seafood restaurants, with a menu based on sustainably sourced fish. Take an octopus-inspired seat at the curved Crustacean Bar and tuck into lobster thermidor or roast shellfish platter. The two-course lunch (noon to 2.30pm) and pre-theatre (5pm to 6.30pm) menu costs £15.

PANCHO VILLA'S
Mexican   ££
☎ 557 4416; www.panchovillas.co.uk; 240 Canongate; ⏱ noon-10pm Mon-Sat, 5-10pm Sun; 🚌 35

With homemade salsa and guacamole, plenty of Latin American staff, and bright colours inspired by the owner's home town of Valle de Bravo, it's not surprising that Pancho's is one of the most authentic-feeling Mexican restaurants in town. It's also great value, with a two-course set lunch for £8.50.

PETIT PARIS French   ££
☎ 226 2442; 38-40 Grassmarket; ⏱ noon-3pm & 5.30-11pm, closed Mon Oct-Mar; 🚌 2

Like the name says, this is a little piece of Paris, complete with checked tablecloths, friendly waiters and good-value grub – the moules marinières (mussels in white wine) are excellent.

TOWER Scottish   £££
☎ 225 3003; Museum of Scotland, Chambers St; ⏱ noon-11pm; 🚌 2, 23, 27, 35, 41 or 42

Decked out in black leather, purple suede and brushed steel, and perched atop the Museum of Scotland building, this sleek, chic restaurant has played host to countless celebrities, from Joanna Lumley to Catherine Zeta-Jones. Grand views of the castle are accompanied by a menu of top-quality Scottish produce, simply prepared – try half a dozen Scottish oysters followed by a char-grilled Aberdeen Angus fillet steak. The two-course pre-theatre menu (5pm to 6.30pm) costs £15.

NEIGHBOURHOODS

OLD TOWN

Candlelight, oak panels and juicy steak at Witchery by the Castle

 WITCHERY BY THE CASTLE
Scottish/French £££
☎ 225 5613; Castlehill, Royal Mile;
⏲ noon-4pm & 5.30-11.30pm; 🚌 2, 23, 27, 41 or 42
Set in a merchant's town house dating from 1595, the Witchery is a candlelit corner of antique splendour with oak-panelled walls, low ceilings, opulent wall hangings and red leather upholstery; stairs lead down to a second, even more romantic, dining room called the Secret Garden. The menu ranges from *foie gras* to Aberdeen Angus steak and the wine list runs to almost 1000 bins.

DRINK

🍸 **ASSEMBLY BAR** *Bar*
☎ 220 4288; www.assemblybar.co.uk; 41 Lothian St; ⏲ noon-1am; 🚌 2, 41 or 42
Assembly originally opened in 1996 (as Iguana), making it positively prehistoric for a style bar, but a combination of timeless decor, cool sounds, big sofas and good-value food has kept it popular. There's a relaxed crowd of mostly students topping up on coffee during the day, but the atmosphere heats up as pre-clubbers pour in during the evening.

BEEHIVE INN *Pub*
☎ 225 7171; 18-20 Grassmarket;
⏲ 11am-midnight Mon-Thu, to 1am Fri & Sat, to 10pm Sun; 🚌 2

The historic Beehive – a former coaching inn – is a big, buzzing party pub serving a range of real ales, but the main attraction is sitting out the back in the Grassmarket's only beer garden, with views up to the castle. The Beehive is the starting point for the Edinburgh Literary Pub Tour (p161).

BOW BAR *Pub*
☎ 226 7667; 80 West Bow; ⏲ noon-11.30pm Mon-Sat, 12.30-11pm Sun; 🚌 2, 23, 27, 41 or 42

A busy, traditional-style pub, unspoilt by touristy trappings, the Bow Bar serves a range of excellent real ales and a vast selection of malt whiskies: this is not the sort of place to go asking for Bacardi Breezers. There are snug window seats and leather benches, but it's often standing room only on Friday and Saturday evenings.

ECCO VINO *Wine Bar*
☎ 225 1441; 19 Cockburn St; ⏲ noon-midnight Mon-Thu, noon-1am Fri & Sat, 12.30pm-midnight Sun; 🚌 all South Bridge buses

With outdoor tables on sunny afternoons, and cosy candlelit intimacy in the evenings, this comfortably cramped Tuscan-style wine bar offers a tempting range of Italian wines, though only a few are available by the glass – best to share a bottle.

JOLLY JUDGE *Pub*
☎ 225 2669; www.jollyjudge.co.uk; 7a James Court; ⏲ noon-midnight Mon & Thu-Sat, noon-11pm Tue & Wed, 12.30-11pm Sun; 🚌 2, 23, 27, 41 or 42; 📶

Tucked away down an Old Town close, the Judge exudes a cosy 17th-century ambience with its low, timber-beamed, painted ceilings and numerous nooks and crannies. The convivial atmosphere is undisturbed by TV, music or gambling machines, and has the added attraction of a log fire in cold weather.

MALT SHOVEL *Pub*
☎ 225 6843; 11-15 Cockburn St; ⏲ 11am-midnight Mon-Thu, 11am-1am Fri & Sat, 12.30pm-midnight Sun; 🚌 all South Bridge buses

A traditional-looking pub, with dark wood and subdued tartanry, the Malt Shovel offers a good range of real ales and more than 100 malt whiskies, and is famed for its regular Tuesday-night jazz and Thursday-night folk-music sessions.

ROYAL MILE TAVERN *Pub*
☎ 557 9681; 127 High St; ⏲ 11am-midnight Mon-Fri, 11am-1am Sat, 12.30pm-11pm Sun; 🚌 35

Punters at the White Hart Inn

An elegant, traditional Edinburgh bar lined with polished wood, brass and mirrors, the Royal Mile serves real ale, good wines and decent pub grub – fish and chips, steak and Guinness pie, sausage and mash etc.

ⓨ VILLAGER *Bar*
☎ 226 2781; 49-50 George IV Bridge; ◷ noon-1am; ▦ 2, 23, 27, 41 or 42
Designed as a cross between a traditional pub and a style bar, the Villager has friendly staff, welcoming regulars and a comfortable, laid-back vibe. It can be standing room only in the main bar in the evenings (the cocktails are excellent), but the side room, with its brown leather sofas and sub-tropical pot plants, comes into its own for a lazy Sunday afternoon with the papers.

ⓨ WHITE HART INN *Pub*
☎ 226 2806; 34 Grassmarket; ◷ 11am-1am; ▦ 2
A brass plaque outside this pub proclaims: 'In the White Hart Inn Robert Burns stayed during his last visit to Edinburgh, 1791.' Claiming to be the city's oldest pub in continuous use (since 1516), it also hosted William Wordsworth in 1803. Not surprisingly, it's a traditional, cosy, low-raftered place. It has folk/acoustic music sessions seven nights a week.

PLAY

⭐ BEDLAM THEATRE *Comedy*
☎ 225 9893; www.bedlamtheatre.co
.uk; 11b Bristo Pl; admission £5; 🚌 2,
23, 27, 41 or 42
The Bedlam hosts a long-
established (more than 10 years)
weekly improvisation slot, the
Improverts, which is hugely popular with local students. Shows kick
off at 10.30pm every Friday, and
you're guaranteed a robust and
entertaining evening.

⭐ BONGO CLUB *Club*
☎ 558 7604; www.thebongoclub.co.uk;
Moray House, Paterson's Land, 37
Holyrood Rd; 🚌 35
During the day the weird and
wonderful Bongo Club offers a cafe-
bar and exhibition space. At night
it transforms into one of the city's
coolest club venues; it also hosts
live music, theatre, cabaret, and
'any other art form'. It's home to Big
N Bashy, a Saturday night club dedicated to reggae, grime, dubstep
and jungle. Also worth checking
out is the booming bass of roots
and dub reggae night Messenger
Sound System (boasting 'a sound
system that could knock you out').

⭐ CABARET VOLTAIRE *Club*
☎ 220 6176; www.thecabaretvoltaire
.com; 36 Blair St; 🚌 35

An atmospheric warren of stone-
lined vaults houses Edinburgh's
most 'alternative' club, which
eschews huge dance floors and
egotistical DJ-worship in favour
of a 'creative crucible' hosting
an eclectic mix of DJs, live acts,
comedy, theatre, visual arts and
the spoken word. It is well worth
a look.

⭐ CAVES *Club*
☎ 557 8989; www.thecavesedinburgh
.com; 8-12 Niddry St South; 🚌 35
A spectacular subterranean club
venue set in the ancient stone
vaults beneath the South Bridge,
the Caves stages a series of one-
off club nights – check the What's
On link on the website for upcom-
ing events

⭐ DANCE BASE *Dance*
☎ 225 5525; www.dancebase.co.uk;
14-16 Grassmarket; ⏰ 8am-9.30pm
Mon-Fri, 10am-5.45pm Sat; 🚌 2
Scotland's National Centre for
Dance is a complex of studios
housed in a spectacular modern
building in the shadow of
Edinburgh Castle; it's actually
worth a visit for the architecture
alone. The centre runs courses in
all kinds of imaginable dance –
from ballroom to belly, hip-hop
to Highland, tango to tap – as
well as hosting workshops and
performances.

⭐ JAZZ BAR *Jazz*
☎ 220 4298; www.thejazzbar.co.uk; 1a Chambers St; admission free-£5; ⏱ 5pm-3am Mon-Fri, 2.30pm-3am Sat, 8pm-3am Sun; 🚌 all South Bridge buses; 📶

This atmospheric cellar bar, with its polished parquet floors, bare stone walls, candlelit tables and stylish steel-framed chairs, is owned and operated by jazz musicians. There's live music every night from 9pm to 3am, and on Saturday from 3pm.

⭐ LIQUID ROOM
Club/Live Music
☎ 225 2564; www.liquidroom.com; 9c Victoria St; ⏱ from 7pm; 🚌 2, 23, 27, 41 or 42

Set in a subterranean vault deep beneath Victoria St, the Liquid Room is a superb live music and club venue with a thundering sound system. There are regular club nights Wednesday to Saturday – the long-running Evol (admission £5; Friday from 10.30pm) is an Edinburgh institution catering to the indie-kid crowd. Regularly voted as Scotland's top club night out.

⭐ OPIUM *Club*
☎ 225 8382; 71 Cowgate; admission free; ⏱ 10pm-3am; 🚌 2 or 35

This traditionally grungy venue in the tunnel-like trench of central Cowgate houses the dark and stylish Opium, the city's top rock club.

Friday and Saturday nights are a thrash-fest of alternative rock and indie, while the popular Apocalypse on Wednesday is a mix of goth, punk and metal.

⭐ PLEASANCE CABARET BAR
Folk
☎ 556 6550; www.pleasance.co.uk; 60 The Pleasance; admission £7; ⏱ 8-11pm Wed; 🚌 35

Home to the Edinburgh Folk Club (www.edinburghfolkclub.co.uk), which runs a programme of visiting bands and singers at 8pm on Wednesdays; there's no advance booking, so buy your ticket at the door. The bar is a major Fringe venue, so there are no concerts here during the Festival period.

⭐ RED VODKA CLUB *Club*
☎ 225 1757; www.redvodkaclub.co.uk; 73 Cowgate; ⏱ 9pm-3am Thu-Sun; 🚌 2 or 35

Red is a stylish, dimly lit, cellarlike venue with a bar that specialises in flavoured and frozen vodkas. Pretty much every night is a club night, with drinks promos during the week; Fridays focus on house music, Saturdays are for R'n'B.

⭐ ROYAL OAK *Folk*
☎ 557 2976; www.royal-oak-folk.com; 1 Infirmary St; admission free; ⏱ 11am-2am Mon-Sat, 12.30pm-2am Sun; 🚌 all South Bridge buses

The ever-popular Royal Oak rivals Sandy Bell's (below) as Edinburgh's most popular folk venue, with music every night in both the public bar and lounge. Admission to the tiny downstairs lounge is free but by ticket only, so get there early if you want to be sure of a place. Sunday-night gigs (8.30pm), organised by the Wee Folk Club, cost £4.

⭐ SANDY BELL'S *Folk*
☎ 225 2751; 25 Forrest Rd; admission free; 🕐 11.30am-12.45am Mon-Sat, 12.30-11pm Sun; 🚌 2, 23, 27, 41 or 42
This unassuming, wood-panelled pub has been a stalwart of the traditional music scene in Edinburgh since The Corrs were in nappies. There's folk music almost every evening at 9pm, and from 3pm Saturday and Sunday.

⭐ STUDIO 24 *Club*
☎ 558 3758; www.studio24edinburgh .co.uk; 24 Calton Rd; 🚌 35
Studio 24 is the dark heart of Edinburgh's underground music scene, with a programme that covers all bases from house to nu-metal via punk, ska, reggae, crossover, tribal, electro, techno and dance. Mission (admission £6; Saturday from 11pm) is the city's classic hard rock, metal and alt night.

Folk music at the White Hart Inn (p60)

⭐ WHISTLE BINKIE'S
Live Music
☎ 557 5114; www.whistlebinkies.com; 4-6 South Bridge; admission free; 🕐 7pm-3am; 🚌 all South Bridge buses
This crowded cellar bar just off the Royal Mile has live music, including rock, blues and folk, every night of the week. Open-mic night on Monday and breaking bands on Tuesday are showcases for new talent – check the website for what's on when.

>HOLYROOD & ARTHUR'S SEAT

Facing the imposing Palace of Holyroodhouse at the foot of the Royal Mile, the once near-derelict district at the foot of the Royal Mile (formerly occupied by a brewery) has been transformed by the construction of the new Scottish Parliament Building, the Our Dynamic Earth tourist attraction, modern offices for the *Scotsman* newspaper and the dramatic Tun Building, which houses BBC Scotland's TV and radio studios.

Holyrood Park, stretching to the south of Holyrood and dominated by the miniature mountain of Arthur's Seat, allows Edinburghers to enjoy a little bit of wilderness in the heart of the city. A former hunting ground of Scottish monarchs, the park covers 650 acres of varied landscape, including crags, moorland and lochs.

The most dramatic feature of the park is the long, curving sweep of Salisbury Crags. The stony path along the foot of the crags is known as the Radical Rd, built in 1820 at the suggestion of Sir Walter Scott to give work to unemployed weavers (from whose politics it took its name). The path makes a good short walk from Holyrood, with fine views over the Old Town.

HOLYROOD & ARTHUR'S SEAT

◎ SEE

Arthur's Seat **1** B4
Duddingston Parish
   Church **2** D5
Duddingston Village **3** D5
Holyrood Abbey **4** A2
Our Dynamic Earth **5** A3
Palace of
   Holyroodhouse **6** A2
Queen's Gallery **7** A2
Scottish Parliament
   Building **8** A3
St Anthony's Chapel **9** B3

⑪ EAT

Foodies at Holyrood **10** A3
Rhubarb **11** C6

▼ DRINK

Sheep Heid **12** D5

SEE

ARTHUR'S SEAT

The rocky peak of Arthur's Seat (251m), carved by ice sheets from the deeply eroded stump of a long-extinct volcano, is a distinctive feature of Edinburgh's skyline. The view from the summit is worth the hike, extending from the Forth Bridges in the west to the distant conical hill of North Berwick Law in the east, with the Ochil Hills and the Highlands on the northwestern horizon.

DUDDINGSTON VILLAGE
🚌 42

Nestling under the southeastern slopes of Arthur's Seat, the picturesque village of Duddingston is one of the oldest parts of the city, dating from the 12th century, though all that remains of that era are parts of the parish church (right). At the western end of the village stands an 18th-century pub, the Sheep Heid (p71), and at the eastern end is Prince Charlie's Cottage, where the Young Pretender held a council of war before the Battle of Prestonpans in 1745.

DUDDINGSTON PARISH CHURCH
Old Church Lane, Duddingston Village;
🚌 42

Poised on a promontory overlooking Duddingston Loch, this church is one of the oldest buildings in Edinburgh, with some interesting medieval relics at the kirkyard gate: the Joug, a metal collar that was used, like the stocks, to tether criminals and sinners, and the Loupin-On Stane, a stone step to help gouty and corpulent parishioners get onto their horses. The early-19th-century watchtower inside the gate was built to deter body-snatchers (p152).

URBAN HILL WALKING IN HOLYROOD PARK

To climb Arthur's Seat from Holyrood, cross Queen's Dr and follow the path that slants leftwards up the hillside beneath the northern end of Salisbury Crags, heading towards the ruins of St Anthony's Chapel, then turn south on a rough path that follows the floor of a shallow dip just east of Long Row Crags. The path eventually curves around to the left and rises more steeply up some steps to a saddle; turn right here and climb to the rocky summit of Arthur's Seat. After taking in the view, descend eastwards to Dunsapie Loch, turn right and follow the road for about 200m then descend to the left on the steep steps known as Jacob's Ladder. At the bottom, turn left into Duddingston village and reward yourself with a pint at the Sheep Heid pub (p71).

View of Arthur's Seat (p66) from Edinburgh Castle

● HOLYROOD ABBEY

Horse Wynd; admission via Palace of Holyroodhouse; ☽ **10am-6pm Jul & Aug, 10am-5pm Apr-Jun, Sep & Oct, 10am-5pm Wed-Sun Nov-Mar, last admission 70min before closing;** 🚍 **35 or 36**

Founded in 1128 by King David I, this ancient abbey was probably named after a fragment of the True Cross (*rood* is an old Scots word for cross) said to have been brought to Scotland by David's mother, St Margaret. The bay on the right, as you look at the huge, arched, eastern window, is the royal burial vault, which holds the remains of Kings David II, James II and James V, and of Mary Queen of Scots' husband, Lord Darnley.

● OUR DYNAMIC EARTH

☎ **550 7800; www.dynamicearth .co.uk; Holyrood Rd; adult/child £10.50/7;** ☽ **10am-6pm Jul & Aug, 10am-5.30pm Apr-Jun, Sep & Oct, 10am-5pm Wed-Sun Nov-Mar, last admission 90min before closing;** 🚍 **36;** ♿ 🚻

Billed as an interactive, multi-media journey of discovery through earth's history from the Big Bang to the present day, Dynamic Earth is hugely popular with kids of all ages. It's a slick extravaganza of hi-tech special effects cleverly designed to fire up young minds with curiosity about all things geological and environmental. (Its true purpose, of course, is to disgorge you into

MYSTERY OF THE MINIATURE COFFINS

In July 1836 five boys hunting for rabbits on the slopes of Arthur's Seat made a strange discovery: in a hollow beneath a rock, arranged on a pile of slates, were 17 tiny wooden coffins. Each was just four inches (10cm) long and contained a roughly carved human figure dressed in handmade clothes.

Many theories have been put forward in explanation, but the most convincing is that the coffins were made in response to the infamous Burke and Hare murders (p152) of 1831–32: the number of coffins matched the number of known victims. It was a common belief that people whose bodies had been dissected by anatomists could not enter the Kingdom of Heaven, and it is thought that someone fashioned the tiny figures in order to provide the murder victims with a form of Christian burial.

Eight of the 17 coffins survive, and can be seen in the National Museum of Scotland (p44). Edinburgh author Ian Rankin makes use of the story of the coffins in his detective novel *The Falls*.

a gift shop stacked with plastic dinosaurs and souvenir T-shirts.)

🅖 PALACE OF HOLYROODHOUSE

☎ 556 5100; www.royalcollection.org
.uk; Horse Wynd; adult/child £10.25/6.20,
joint ticket incl admission to palace
£14.30/8.30; 🕘 9.30am-6pm Apr-Oct,
9.30am-4.30pm Nov-Mar, closed 25 & 26
Dec & during royal visits; 🚌 35 or 36
Mary Queen of Scots spent six
eventful years (1561–67) living at
Holyroodhouse, a 16th-century
tower house that was extended to
create a 17th-century royal palace,
now Her Majesty the Queen's
official residence in Scotland. The
highlight of the guided tour is
Mary Queen of Scots' bed chamber
with its low, painted ceilings and
secret staircase connecting to her

husband Lord Darnley's bedroom.
This was where a jealous Darnley
restrained the pregnant queen
while her henchmen murdered
her secretary – and possible lover
– David Rizzio. In her own words,
they '…dragged David forth with
great cruelty from our cabinet and
at the entrance of our chamber
dealt him 56 dagger blows'. A
plaque in the next room marks the
spot where he bled to death.

🅖 QUEEN'S GALLERY

☎ 556 5100; www.royalcollection.org
.uk; Horse Wynd; adult/child £5.50/3,
joint ticket incl admission to palace
£14.30/8.30; 🕘 9.30am-6pm Apr-Oct,
9.30am-4.30pm Nov-Mar, closed 25 & 26
Dec & during royal visits; 🚌 35 or 36
This stunning modern gallery,
which occupies the shell of a

former church and school, is a showcase for exhibitions of art from the Royal Collections. The exhibitions change every six months or so; for details of the latest, check the website.

⬤ SCOTTISH PARLIAMENT BUILDING

☎ 348 5200; www.scottish.parliament.uk; admission free; 🕒 9am-6.30pm Tue-Thu, 10am-5.30pm Mon & Fri in session, 10am-6pm Mon-Fri in recess Apr-Oct, 10am-4pm in recess Nov-Mar; 🚍 35 or 36; ♿

Edinburgh's most spectacular and controversial building, officially opened in 2004, houses Scotland's devolved parliament.

Built from concrete, steel, oak and granite, it was a flagship architectural project that went way over budget and way over schedule, and was dogged by contention and bad luck at every step. The Main Hall, which houses an exhibition, shop and cafe, and the public gallery overlooking the Debating Chamber are open to the public; alternatively, you can take a free guided tour which includes a visit to the Debating Chamber, a committee room, the Garden Lobby and, if possible, the office of a Member of the Scottish Parliament (MSP). The main visitor entrance is on Horse Wynd.

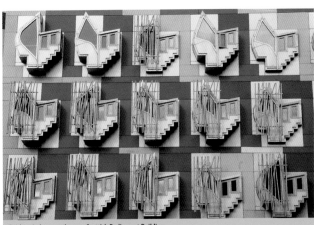

Quirky windows on the new Scottish Parliament Building

DECODING THE SCOTTISH PARLIAMENT BUILDING

Enric Miralles (1955–2000), the architect who conceived the Scottish Parliament Building, believed that a building could be a work of art. However, the weird concrete confection that has sprouted at the foot of Salisbury Crags has left the good people of Edinburgh staring and scratching their heads in confusion. What does it all mean?

First, you have to understand that the site is no less symbolic than the building itself. Holyrood has been a seat of Scottish power, religious and royal, for more than 1000 years – the ruins of Holyrood Abbey (p67) and the Palace of Holyroodhouse (p68) lie just across the road.

Then you have to see the site from above, looking down from Salisbury Crags or Calton Hill. Miralles believed that the building should seem to grow out of the land, a flower of democracy rooted in Scottish soil – the cluster of leaf-shaped roofs appears to blossom at the end of a series of linear earthworks that spread out from Arthur's Seat like the branch of a tree.

The exterior of the building has echoes of the Scottish landscape and architecture in its details. The public entrance opposite the Palace of Holyroodhouse is a wall of polished grey concrete and glass, partly hidden behind a latticed forest of wooden poles, reminiscent of birch woods or fields of barley. The 1st-floor facade to the right, and the towers around to the left, are decorated with unusual, inverted L-shaped panels. These represent a curtain being drawn aside, exposing the workings of government to public scrutiny.

The west wall of the MSP (Member of the Scottish Parliament) Building, which houses the members' individual offices, is covered in quirkily shaped projecting windows, whose outline is said to have been inspired by the silhouette of the *Rev Robert Walker Skating on Duddingston Loch*, one of Scotland's most famous paintings.

The Canongate Wall, which runs alongside the foot of the Royal Mile, is actually a blast-protection wall to guard against potential terrorist car bombings. The attractive design, inlaid with stones from all over Scotland and inscribed with quotations from Scottish literature, was based on a sketch of Edinburgh streets that Miralles made from his hotel window.

The dimly lit Main Hall, inside the public entrance, has a low, arched ceiling like a cave or castle vault. It's the starting point for a metaphorical journey from relative darkness up to the Debating Chamber which is, in contrast, a palace of light – the light of democracy. This magnificent chamber is the centrepiece of the Parliament, designed not to glorify but to humble the politicians who sit within it. The windows face Calton Hill, allowing MSPs to look up to its monuments (reminders of the Scottish Enlightenment), while the massive, pointed oak beams of the roof are suspended by steel threads above the politicans' heads like so many Damoclean swords.

EAT

RHUBARB

Modern Scottish   £££

☎ 225 1333; Prestonfield House Hotel, Priestfield Rd; ⏰ noon-2pm & 6.30-10pm Mon-Sat, 1-3pm & 6.30-10pm Sun
Set in the splendid 17th-century Prestonfield House, Rhubarb is a feast for the eyes as well as the tastebuds. The over-the-top decor of rich reds set off with black and gold and the sensuous surfaces – damask, brocade, marble, gilded leather – that make you want to touch everything are matched by the intense flavours and rich textures of the food. Take your postprandial coffee and brandy upstairs to the sumptuous fireside sofas in the Tapestry and Leather rooms. A two-course lunch menu is available for £17. There is no public transport here.

FOODIES AT HOLYROOD

Cafe   £

☎ 557 6836; www.foodiesatholyrood.com; 67 Holyrood Rd; ⏰ 8am-6pm Mon-Fri, 10am-6pm Sat & Sun; 🚌 35; 📶 👶

This stylish cafe, handy for a post-sightseeing snack after visiting Holyroodhouse or Dynamic Earth, is dedicated to serving top quality, locally sourced produce. Healthy breakfasts range from homemade muesli to porridge with apple, sultanas and cinnamon, while the lunch menu includes soups, freshly prepared sandwiches, ciabattas and baked potatoes.

DRINK

SHEEP HEID   *Pub*

☎ 656 6951; 43-45 The Causeway; ⏰ 11am-11pm Mon-Wed, 11am-midnight Thu-Sat, 12.30-11pm Sun; 🚌 42
Possibly the oldest licensed premises in Edinburgh – dating back to 1360 – the Sheep Heid is more like a country pub than a city bar. Set in the semirural shadow of Arthur's Seat, it's famous for its 19th-century skittles alley and lovely beer garden. The name comes from an ornamental snuff box in the form of a sheep's head that was presented to the inn by James VI in 1580, and is commemorated in a carving which sits above the bar.

>NEW TOWN

In contrast to the maze of tall tenements and narrow wynds that crowd along the Royal Mile, Edinburgh's New Town is a monument to Georgian gentility, a neat and orderly grid of broad streets and elegant town houses. Laid out in the 1760s, the New Town was built to provide

NEW TOWN

◎ SEE
Calton Hill 1 F4
Charlotte Square 2 A5
Edinburgh Printmakers'
    Workshop & Gallery 3 E3
Floral Clock 4 C5
Georgian House 5 A5
Mansfield Place Church ..6 D3
National Gallery of
    Scotland 7 C5
Nelson Monument 8 F4
Old Calton Burial Ground ..9 E5
Princes Street Gardens ..10 B6
Royal Scottish
    Academy 11 C5
Scott Monument 12 D5
Scottish National
    Portrait Gallery 13 D4

🅰 SHOP
Boudiche 14 C5
Crombie's 15 D3
Cruise 16 B5
Fopp 17 C5
Harvey Nichols 18 D4
Jenners 19 D5
Jo Malone 20 B5
Lime Blue 21 B5
McNaughtan's
    Bookshop 22 F2
One World Shop 23 A6
Oscar & Fitch 24 D4
Palenque 25 D3
Q-Store 26 D3
Scottish Gallery 27 C4

Tiso 28 B5
Valvona & Crolla 29 F3
Waterstone's 30 B6
Waterstone's 31 B5
Whistles 32 B5

🍴 EAT
21212 ....33 F4
Bigos 34 G1
Blue Moon Café .... (see 26)
Café Marlayne 35 B5
Café Royal Oyster Bar ..36 D5
Centotre .... (see 32)
Circle 37 C2
Dogs 38 B4
Dome Grill Room 39 D5
Escargot Bleu 40 D3
Fishers in the City 41 C5
Forth Floor Restaurant &
    Brasserie .... (see 18)
Hadrian's Brasserie 42 D5
Henderson's Salad
    Table 43 C4
Howie's 44 E4
La P'tite Folie 45 B4
L'Artichaut 46 C2
Locanda de Gusti 47 D3
Mussel Inn 48 C5
Number One 49 D5
Oloroso 50 B5
Stac Polly 51 D3
Urban Angel 52 C4
Valvona &
    Crolla Caffé Bar ...... (see 29)
Valvona &
    Crolla Vincaffé 53 D4

🍸 DRINK
Abbotsford 54 D5
Amicus Apple .... (see 14)
Basement 55 E4
Bramble 56 B4
Café Royal
    Circle Bar .... (see 36)
Cask & Barrel 57 D3
Clark's Bar 58 B3
Cumberland Bar 59 C3
Elbow 60 D1
Guildford Arms 61 D5
Joseph Pearce's 62 F3
Kay's Bar 63 B4
Kenilworth 64 B5
Mathers 65 E4
Oloroso Lounge Bar .. (see 50)
Oxford Bar 66 B5
Regent 67 H4
Robertsons 37 ....68 C5
Tigerlily 69 A5
Tonic 70 B5

★ PLAY
CC Blooms 71 E3
Edinburgh Playhouse 72 E4
Jam House 73 C4
Lulu .... (see 69)
Opal Lounge 74 C5
Stand Comedy Club 75 D4
Voodoo Rooms .... (see 36)
Vue Cinema 76 E4

Please see over for map

healthier, more spacious living quarters for the city's wealthy citizens, with some of its finest neoclassical architecture designed by Robert Adam.

Today the New Town remains the world's most complete and unspoilt example of Georgian architecture and town planning; along with the Old Town, it was declared a Unesco World Heritage Site in 1995. George St – its main axis – was once the centre of Edinburgh's financial district, but now that the big financial firms have relocated to the new Exchange district, the banks and office buildings have been taken over by designer boutiques, trendy bars and clubs and upmarket restaurants.

 # SEE

◉ CALTON HILL
🚌 **all Princes St & North Bridge buses**
Calton Hill, which rises dramatically above the eastern end of Princes St, is Edinburgh's acropolis, its summit scattered with grandiose monuments dating mostly from the first half of the 19th century. It is also one of the best viewpoints in Edinburgh, with a panorama that takes in the castle, Holyrood, Arthur's Seat, the Firth of Forth, New Town and the full length of Princes St. On Regent Rd, on the hill's southern side, is the Burns Monument (1830), a Greek-style memorial to poet Robert Burns.

◉ CHARLOTTE SQUARE
🚌 **all Princes St buses**
At the western end of George St is Charlotte Sq, the architectural jewel of the New Town, which was designed by Robert Adam shortly before his death in 1791. The north-ern side of the square is Adam's masterpiece and one of the finest examples of Georgian architecture anywhere. Bute House, in the centre at No 6, is the official residence of Scotland's first minister.

◉ EDINBURGH PRINTMAKERS' WORKSHOP & GALLERY
☎ **557 2479; www.edinburgh-print makers.co.uk; 23 Union St; admission free;** 🕑 **10am-6pm Tue-Sat, closed 24 Dec-9 Jan;** 🚌 **8 or 17**
Founded in 1967, this was the UK's first 'open-access' printmaking studio, providing studio space and equipment for professional artists and beginners alike. You can watch printmakers at work in the ground-floor studio, while the 1st-floor gal-lery hosts exhibitions of lithographs and screen prints by local artists.

◉ GEORGIAN HOUSE
☎ **226 2160; 7 Charlotte Sq; adult/ child £5.50/4.50;** 🕑 **10am-6pm Jul & Aug, 10am-5pm Apr-Jun, Sep & Oct, 11am-4pm Mar, 11am-3pm Nov;** 🚌 **13, 19, 36, 37 or 41**
Dating from 1796, this elegant town house has been beautifully

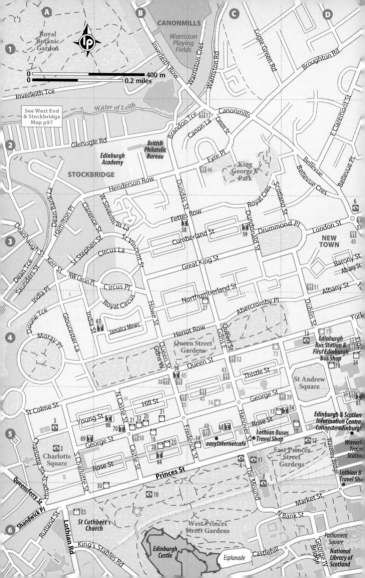

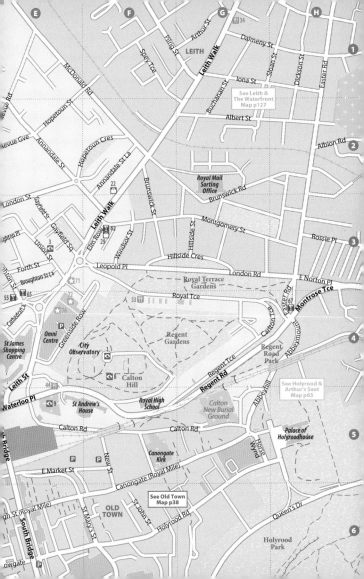

E **F** **G** **H**

1

Arthur St

Ring St

Spey Tce

Dalmeny St

Sloan St

Dickson St

Easter Rd

LEITH

Leith Walk

Iona St

Buchanan St

McDonald Rd

See Leith &
The Waterfront
Map p127

Hopetoun St

Albert St

2

Annandale St

Hopetoun Cres

Annandale St La

Brunswick St

Royal Mail
Sorting
Office

Brunswick Rd

Albion Rd

London St

Gayfield Sq

22

Tayfield Pl

Elm Row

92
29

Windsor St

Hillside St

Montgomery St

Rossie Pl

Union St

Leith Walk

Hillside Cres

London Rd

E Norton Pl

Forth St

Broughton St La

Leopold Pl

71

3

55

65

Cathedral La

26

Greenside Row

Royal Terrace
Gardens

Royal Tce

33

67

Easter Rd

Calton Rd

Montrose Tce

St James
Shopping
Centre

Omni
Centre

City
Observatory
1

Regent
Gardens

Regent
Road Park

Abbeyhill

Blantyre

4

Leith St

44

8

Calton
Hill

Regent Tce

Regem Rd

See Holyrood &
Arthur's Seat
Map p65

Waterloo Pl

9

St Andrew's
House

Royal High
School

Calton
New Burial
Ground

Abbeyhill

Calton Rd

Calton Rd

Calton Rd

Palace of
Holyroodhouse

5

Bridge

E Market St

New St

Canongate
Kirk

Canongate (Royal Mile)

Horse Wynd

See Old Town
Map p38

St Mary's St

S John's St

Holyrood Rd

Holyrood Rd

OLD
TOWN

Queen's Dr

6

South Bridge

gh St (Royal Mile)

owgate

Holyrood
Park

restored to show how Edinburgh's wealthy elite lived at the end of the 18th century. The rooms are furnished with the finest period furniture and the walls are decorated with paintings by Allan Ramsay, Henry Raeburn and Sir Joshua Reynolds. There are costumed guides on hand to add a bit of character, and a 35-minute video presentation helps to bring the place to life.

MANSFIELD PLACE CHURCH

☎ 474 8033; www.mansfieldtraquair .org.uk; Mansfield Pl; admission free; ⏱ 1-4pm 2nd Sun of month, 11am-1pm Sun-Thu during Edinburgh Festival Fringe; 🚌 8, 13 or 17

In contrast to the austerity of most of Edinburgh's religious buildings, the 19th-century neo-Romanesque Mansfield Place Church at the foot of Broughton St contains a remarkable series of Renaissance-style frescoes painted in the 1890s by Irish-born artist Phoebe Anna Traquair (1852–1936).

NATIONAL GALLERY OF SCOTLAND

☎ 624 6200; www.nationalgalleries.org; The Mound; admission free, except for special exhibitions; ⏱ 10am-5pm Fri-Wed, 10am-7pm Thu, noon-5pm 1 Jan, closed 25 & 26 Dec; 🚌 all Princes St buses; ♿

Scotland's premier collection of art is housed in this imposing neoclassical temple that nestles beneath the Old Town skyline. Once a year, in January, the gallery exhibits its collection of Turner watercolours, bequeathed by Henry Vaughan in 1900. See p21 for more details.

NELSON MONUMENT

☎ 556 2716; Calton Hill; admission £3; ⏱ 1-6pm Mon & 10am-6pm Tue-Sat Apr-Sep, 10am-3pm Mon-Sat Oct-Mar; 🚌 all Leith St buses

Looking a bit like an upturned telescope (the similarity is intentional), the Nelson Monument was built to commemorate Admiral Lord Nelson's victory at Trafalgar in 1805. In 1852 a time-ball was added as a time signal for ships anchored in the Firth of Forth – it still drops from the cross-bars of the mast at the top of the monument at 1pm every day. The view from the top is superb.

OLD CALTON BURIAL GROUND

Waterloo Pl; ⏱ 8am-dusk; 🚌 all Princes St buses

One of Edinburgh's many atmospheric old cemeteries, Old Calton is dominated by the tall black obelisk of the Political Martyrs' Monument, which commemorates those who suffered in the fight for electoral reform in the 1790s. In the southern corner is the massive

Getting some sun in the Princes Street Gardens

cylindrical grey stone tomb of David Hume (1711–76), Scotland's most famous philosopher. Hume was a noted atheist, prompting rumours that he had made a Faustian pact with the devil; after his death his friends held a vigil at the tomb for eight nights, burning candles and firing pistols into the darkness lest evil spirits should come to bear away his soul.

◉ PRINCES STREET GARDENS
Princes St; admission free; ☼ **dawn-dusk;** 🚌 **all Princes St buses**
These beautiful gardens lie in a valley that was once occupied by the Nor' Loch (North Loch), a boggy depression that was drained in the early 19th century. They are split in the middle by The Mound – around two million cart-loads of earth dug out from foundations during the construction of the New Town and dumped here to provide a road link across the valley to the Old Town. It was completed in 1830.

In the middle of the western part of the gardens is the Ross Bandstand, a venue for open-air concerts in summer and at Hogmanay, and the stage for the famous Fireworks Concert during the Edinburgh Festival. At the gate beside The Mound is the **Floral Clock**, a working clock laid out in flowers; it was first created in 1903 and the design changes every year.

THE DAILY BANG

On Princes St you can tell locals and visitors apart by their reaction to the sudden explosion that rips through the air each day at one o'clock. Locals check their watches, while visitors shy like startled ponies. It's the One O'Clock Gun, fired from Mills Mount Battery on the castle battlements at 1pm sharp every day except Sunday. From 1979 until his death in 2005 it was fired by District Gunner Sgt Thomas McKay (known as Tam the Gun); it is now in the hands of Sgt James Shannon (inevitably nicknamed Shannon the Cannon).

The gun's origins date from the mid-19th century, when the accurate setting of a ship's chronometer was essential for safe navigation. The city authorities installed a time-signal on top of the Nelson Monument (p76) that was visible to ships anchored in the Firth of Forth. The gun was added as an audible signal that could be used when rain or mist obscured the ball. An interesting little exhibition in the Museum of Edinburgh (p44) details the gun's history and workings.

ROYAL SCOTTISH ACADEMY

☎ 225 6671; www.royalscottish academy.org; The Mound; admission free, except for special exhibitions; 10am-5pm Mon-Sat, 2-5pm Sun; all Princes St buses

The distinguished Greek Doric temple located at the corner of The Mound and Princes St, designed by William Playfair and built between 1823 and 1836, houses a collection of paintings, sculptures and architectural drawings by academy members dating from 1831, and also hosts temporary exhibitions throughout the year – details are posted on the website.

SCOTT MONUMENT

☎ 529 4068; E Princes Street Gardens; admission £3; 10am-7pm Apr-Sep, 9am-4pm Mon-Sat, 10am-4pm Sun Oct-Mar; all Princes St buses

The massive Gothic spire of the Scott Monument was built by public subscription in memory of novelist Sir Walter Scott after his death in 1832. You can climb the 287 steps to the top for a superb view of the city; the stone figures that decorate the niches on the monument represent characters from Scott's novels. The statue of Scott with his favourite deerhound, Maida, was carved from a single 30-tonne block of white Italian marble.

SCOTTISH NATIONAL PORTRAIT GALLERY

☎ 624 6200; www.nationalgalleries .org; 1 Queen St; admission free; 10am-5pm Fri-Wed, 10am-7pm Thu; all York Pl buses

The galleries in this Venetian Gothic palace depict Scottish history through portraits and sculptures of famous Scottish personalities, from

Robert Burns and Bonnie Prince Charlie to Sean Connery and Billy Connolly. It also houses the National Photography Collection, which includes works by David Octavius Hill and Robert Adamson, the 19th-century Scottish pioneers of portrait photography.

SHOP

BOUDICHE *Lingerie*
☎ 226 5255; www.boudiche.com; 15 Frederick St; 10am-6pm Mon-Wed, Fri & Sat, 10am-7pm Thu, noon-5pm Sun; all Princes St buses

Boudiche is a divinely decadent boudoir designed to make shopping for lingerie a lush, leisurely experience – you can try on basques and bustiers in the opulent changing rooms, each one equipped with a mirrored dressing table and an antique bell to call for a shop attendant.

CROMBIE'S *Food & Drink*
☎ 557 0111; www.sausages.co.uk; 97-101 Broughton St; 8am-6pm Mon-Fri, 8am-5pm Sat; 8 or 17

Crombie's is a top-quality butcher shop where the good folk of Edinburgh go to stock up on prime Scottish beef and lamb, and superb homemade haggis. It's also famous for its gourmet sausages, with almost three dozen varieties ranging from wild boar and apricot to basil, beef and blackberry.

CRUISE *Fashion*
☎ 226 3524; 94 George St; 10am-6pm Mon-Fri, 9.30am-6pm Sat, noon-5pm Sun; 13, 19, 37 or 41

An ornately corniced and plastered foyer leads into three floors of white-painted, minimalist art-gallery-like decor. This and a second outlet at nearby 80 George St show off the best of mainstream designer labels for men and women including Paul Smith, Jasper Conran, Hugo Boss, Joseph Tricot, Armani and Dolce & Gabbana.

FOPP *Music*
☎ 220 0310; 7 Rose St; 9.30am-7pm Mon-Sat, 11am-6pm Sun; all Princes St buses

Fopp grew from a one-man record stall in Glasgow into the UK's largest independent music store, before being bought out by HMV in 2007. It's still a good place to hunt for cheap CDs and vinyl, and the friendly staff really know what they're talking about.

HARVEY NICHOLS *Department Store*
☎ 524 8388; www.harveynichols.com; 30-34 St Andrew Sq; 10am-6pm Mon-Wed, 10am-8pm Thu, 10am-7pm Fri & Sat, 11am-6pm Sun; all St Andrew Sq buses

Harvey Nicks is as famous for its eye-popping pricetags as for its range of world-famous brand names. The Edinburgh store offers four floors of designer labels, from Prada shades to Paul Smith suits, via lingerie, luggage, hats and handbags.

JENNERS *Department Store*

225 2442; www.houseoffraser.co.uk; 48 Princes St; 9.30am-6pm Mon-Wed, Fri & Sat, 9.30am-8pm Thu, 11am-6pm Sun; all Princes St buses

Founded in 1838, Jenners is the grande dame of Edinburgh shopping, and Britain's oldest department store. Its labyrinthine five floors stock a wide range of quality goods, both classic and contemporary – it's especially strong on designer shoes and handbags, hats, knitwear and Oriental rugs – and includes a food hall, a hairdresser, a gift-wrapping service and four cafes.

JO MALONE *Cosmetics*

478 8555; www.jomalone.co.uk; 93 George St; 10am-6pm Mon-Wed, 10am-7pm Thu, 9.30am-6pm Fri & Sat, noon-5pm Sun; 13, 19, 37 or 41

This sweet-smelling palace of posh cosmetics has in-store experts offering a 'fragrance-combining' consultation that will allow you to choose your perfect perfume, along with a range of other scents to 'layer' over it. Try the original nutmeg and ginger bath oil that made Ms Malone famous, or other intriguing combinations such as lime, basil and mandarin, or amber and lavender.

LIME BLUE *Jewellery*

220 2164; www.lime-blue.co.uk; 107 George St; 10am-6pm Mon-Wed & Fri, 10am-7pm Thu, noon-5pm Sun; 13, 19, 37 or 41

Put on your shades and tighten your grip on that purse – you'll be dazzled by both the merchandise and the pricetags in this elegant and clean-cut jewellery emporium, with diamond-encrusted necklaces and rings by Leo Pizzo, finely crafted brooches by Picchiotti and watches by Versace. Downstairs you'll find a broad range of silver jewellery, crystalware and other luxury goods.

MCNAUGHTAN'S BOOKSHOP *Books*

556 5897; www.mcnaughtansbookshop.com; 3a-4a Haddington Pl; 11am-5pm Tue-Sat; all Leith Walk buses

The maze of shelves at McNaughtan's bookshop – established in 1957 – houses a broad spectrum of general second-hand and antiquarian books, with good selections of Scottish, history, travel, art and architecture, and children's books.

☐ ONE WORLD SHOP
Arts & Crafts

☎ 229 4541; www.oneworldshop
.co.uk; St John's Church, Princes St;
🕑 10am- 5.30pm Mon-Sat &
noon-5pm Sun, to 6pm daily Aug; 🚌 all
Princes St buses

The One World Shop sells a wide range of handmade crafts from developing countries, including paper goods, rugs, textiles, jewellery, ceramics, accessories, food and drink, all from accredited Fair Trade suppliers. During the Festival period (when the shop stays open till 6pm) there's a crafts fair in the churchyard outside.

☐ OSCAR & FITCH *Glasses*

☎ 556 6461; www.oscarandfitch.com;
20 Multrees Walk; 🕑 10am-6pm Mon-
Wed, Fri & Sat, 10am-7pm Thu, 11am-
5pm Sun; 🚌 all St Andrew Sq buses

If you're looking for some stylish spectacles, this boutique stocks the city's largest selection of designer eyewear, from head-turningly avant-garde daytime glasses to popstar-cool shades, all expertly fitted to your personal satisfaction.

☐ PALENQUE *Jewellery*

☎ 225 7194; www.palenquejewellery
.co.uk; 99 Rose St; 🕑 10am-5.30pm
Mon-Sat; 🚌 all Princes St buses

Another branch of the Old Town jewellery shop (p51).

☐ Q-STORE *Gay & Lesbian*

☎ 477 4756; 5 Barony St; 🕑 11am-7pm
Mon-Fri, 11am-6pm Sat, 1-5pm Sun;
🚌 8 or 17

Next door to the Blue Moon Café (p83), the Q-Store is a gay and lesbian shop selling books, mags, videos, DVDs, sex toys, naughty underwear and clubbing gear.

☐ SCOTTISH GALLERY
Arts & Crafts

☎ 558 1200; www.scottish-gallery.co
.uk; 16 Dundas St; 🕑 10am-6pm Mon-
Fri, 10am-4pm Sat; 🚌 23 or 27

Home to Edinburgh's leading art dealers, Aitken Dott, this private gallery exhibits and sells paintings by contemporary Scottish artists and the masters of the late 19th and early 20th centuries (including the Scottish Colourists), as well as a wide range of ceramics, glassware, jewellery and textiles.

☐ TISO *Sports*

☎ 225 9486; www.tiso.com; 123-125
Rose St; 🕑 9.30am-5.30pm Mon, Tue,
Fri & Sat, 10am-5.30pm Wed, 9.30am-
7.30pm Thu, 11am-5pm Sun; 🚌 all
Princes St buses

Founded by the late Scottish mountaineer Graham Tiso, Edinburgh's biggest outdoor-equipment store offer four floors of camping, hiking, climbing, canoeing, skiing and snowboarding gear.

☐ VALVONA & CROLLA
Food & Drink

☎ 556 6066; www.valvonacrolla.co.uk;
19 Elm Row; ⏱ 8.30am-6pm Mon-Thu,
8am-6.30pm Fri & Sat, 10.30am-4pm Sun;
🚌 all Leith Walk buses

The acknowledged queen of Edinburgh delicatessens, established during the 1930s, Valvona & Crolla is packed with Mediterranean goodies, including an excellent choice of fine wines. It also has a good cafe (p88).

☐ WATERSTONE'S *Books*

☎ 226 2666; 128 Princes St; ⏱ 8.30am-8pm Mon-Sat, 10.30am-7pm Sun; 🚌 all Princes St buses

Waterstone's flagship Princes St branch has four floors of books, with a good Scottish section on the ground floor and lots of travel guides and a coffee shop on the 2nd floor; it also hosts frequent book signings and author events. There's another **branch** (⏱ 9am-8pm Mon-Fri, 9am-7pm Sat, 10am-7pm Sun) down the road at No 13.

☐ WATERSTONE'S *Books*

☎ 225 3436; 83 George St; ⏱ 9am-7pm Mon-Sat, 11am-6pm Sun;; 🚌 all Princes St buses

The George St branch of the major bookshop.

☐ WHISTLES *Fashion*

☎ 226 4398; 97 George St; ⏱ 10am-6pm Mon-Wed, Fri & Sat, 10am-7pm noon-5pm Sun; 🚌 all Princes St buses

Crisp white and hot pink décor sets off the racks of designer clothes for women in this branch of the well-known London-based store. Lots of little black dresses here – just the place if you're looking for something a little more formal for that special occasion – as well as quirky and off-beat styles.

Delectable delicatessen goods at Valvona & Crolla

⛶ EAT

⛶ 21212 *French* £££

☎ 523 1030; www.21212restaurant
.co.uk; 3 Royal Tce; ☽ noon-1.45pm
& 7-9.30pm Tue-Sat; 🚌 all London Rd
buses

A grand Georgian town house
on the side of Calton Hill is the
elegant setting for Edinburgh's
newest Michelin star. Divine decor
by Timorous Beasties and Ralph
Lauren provide the backdrop to an
exquisitely prepared five-course
dinner (£65 a head) that includes
delights such as baby turbot
poached in olive oil with saffron
pancake, and lamb and merguez
kebab with banana and cucumber
confit.

⛶ BIGOS *Polish* ££

☎ 554 6539; www.e-bigos.co.uk; 277
Leith Walk; ☽ noon-9pm Sun-Thu, to
11pm Fri & Sat; 🚌 all Leith Walk buses

Any twinge of homesickness felt
by members of Edinburgh's Polish
community is rapidly dispelled at
this rustic haunt halfway down
Leith Walk. The restaurant's
signature dish, *bigos*, is classic
Polish comfort food – a slow-
cooked stew of cabbage, sausage,
meat and mushrooms. The rest of
the menu is similarly hearty and
filling, from potato pancakes to
goulash and dumplings. Bigos is
BYOB, so pick up a couple of bot-

tles of Zywiec beer at the nearby
Polish deli.

⛶ BLUE MOON CAFÉ *Cafe* £

☎ 557 0911; www.bluemooncafe.co.uk;
1 Barony St; ☽ 10am-10pm; 🚌 8 or
17; Ⓥ

The Blue Moon is the focus of
Broughton St's gay social life –
always busy, always friendly, and
serving up tasty nachos, salads,
sandwiches and baked potatoes.
It's famous for its homemade
burgers (beef, chicken or falafel),
which come with a range of
toppings, and delicious daily
specials.

⛶ CAFÉ MARLAYNE *French* ££

☎ 226 2230; 76 Thistle St; ☽ noon-2pm
& 6-10pm daily; 🚌 13, 24, 29 or 42

All weathered wood and warm
yellow walls, this bistro is a cosy
little nook offering satisfying
French farmhouse cooking –
brandade de morue with green
salad, slow roast rack of lamb,
boudin noir (black pudding) with
scallops and sautéed potato – at
very reasonable prices. It's small,
so book a table well in advance.

⛶ CAFÉ ROYAL OYSTER BAR
French/Seafood £££

☎ 556 4124; 17a W Register St; ☽ noon-
2pm & 7-10pm; 🚌 all Princes St buses

Pass through the revolving doors
here and you're transported back
to Victorian times – a palace of

glinting mahogany, polished brass, marble floors, stained glass, Doulton tiles, gilded cornices and table linen so thick that it creaks when you fold it. The menu is mostly classic seafood, from oysters on ice to succulent *coquilles St Jacques Parisienne* (scallops in a cream and mushroom sauce).

CENTOTRE *Italian* ££-£££

☎ 225 1550; www.centotre.com; 103 George St; ⏰ 7.30am-midnight Mon-Sat, 10am-10pm Sun; 🚌 all Princes St buses; 📶 🚼

A palatial Georgian banking hall enlivened with fuchsia-pink banners and aubergine booths is home to this lively, child-friendly Italian bar and restaurant, where the emphasis is on fresh, authentic ingredients (produce imported weekly from Milan, homemade bread and pasta), and uncomplicated enjoyment of food.

CIRCLE *Cafe* £

☎ 624 4666; 1 Brandon Tce; ⏰ 8.30am-5pm Mon-Sat, 9am-4.30pm Sun; 🚌 13, 17 or 36; Ⓥ

A great place for breakfast or a good-value lunch, Circle is a bustling neighbourhood cafe serving great coffee and cakes, and fresh, tasty lunch dishes ranging from home-baked quiches to smoked haddock and poached egg hollandaise.

DOME GRILL ROOM
International £££

☎ 624 8624; www.thedomeedinburgh.com; 14 George St; ⏰ noon-10pm Sun-Wed, to 11pm Thu-Sat; 🚌 24, 28 or 45

Housed in a magnificent former banking hall, with a lofty glass-domed ceiling, pillared arches and a mosaic-tiled floor, the Dome Grill Room boasts one of Edinburgh's most impressive dining rooms. The menu here holds few surprises – from smoked salmon to chargrilled chicken or roast lamb – but it's really the setting that sells the place; it's hard to keep your eyes on your plate with all the stupendous finery that surrounds you.

ESCARGOT BLEU *French* ££

☎ 556 1600; www.lescargotbleu.co.uk; 56 Broughton St; ⏰ noon-3pm & 5.30-10pm; 🚌 8 or 17

As with its companion restaurant, l'Escargot Blanc (p103), this cute little bistro is as Gallic as garlic but makes fine use of quality Scottish produce in its menu – the French-speaking staff will knowledgeably lead you through a menu that includes authentic Savoyard *tartiflette*, *quenelle* of pike with lobster sauce, and pigs' cheeks braised in red wine with roast winter vegetables.

FISHERS IN THE CITY
Seafood ££-£££

☎ 225 5109; www.fishersbistros.co.uk; 58 Thistle St; ⏰ noon-10.30pm; 🚌 13, 19, 37 or 41

This more sophisticated version of the famous Fishers Bistro in Leith (p132), with its granite-topped tables, warm yellow walls and a nautical theme, specialises in superior Scottish seafood – the knowledgeable staff serve up plump and succulent oysters, meltingly sweet scallops, and sea bass that's been grilled to perfection.

FORTH FLOOR RESTAURANT & BRASSERIE
Scottish ££-£££

☎ 524 8350; www.harveynichols.com; 30-34 St Andrew Sq; ⏰ 10am-5pm Mon, 10am-10pm Tue-Sat, 11am-5pm Sun; 🚌 all St Andrew Sq buses

The in-store restaurant at Harvey Nichols has floor-to-ceiling windows overlooking St Andrew Sq, making it a great place to enjoy sunset views. The food has as much designer chic as the surroundings, while the less formal brasserie offers simpler dishes, and also serves Sunday brunch (11am to 5pm).

HADRIAN'S BRASSERIE
Scottish/French ££-£££

☎ 557 5000; www.hadriansbrasserie .com; Balmoral Hotel, 1 Princes St; ⏰ 7-10.30am, noon-2.30pm & 6-10.30pm

Mon-Sat, 7.30-11am, 12.30-3pm & 6-10.30pm Sun; 🚌 all Princes St buses

The brasserie at the Balmoral Hotel has a 1930s feel, with pale-green walls, dark-wood furniture, and waiters with white aprons and black waistcoats. The menu at Hadrian's includes posh versions of popular dishes such as asparagus with rocket and parmesan, haggis with whisky sauce, game terrine with Cumberland jelly, and rib-eye steak with bearnaise sauce.

HENDERSON'S SALAD TABLE *Vegetarian* £

☎ 225 2131; www.hendersonsof edinburgh.co.uk; 94 Hanover St; ⏰ 8am-10.45pm Mon-Sat, Sun during the Edinburgh Festival; 🚌 23 or 27; Ⓥ ♿

Established in 1962, Henderson's is the grandmother of Edinburgh's vegetarian restaurants. The food is mostly organic, guaranteed GM-free, and special dietary requirements can be catered for. The restaurant still has a 1970s feel to it (but in a good way), and the daily salads and hot dishes are as popular as ever. Two-course set lunch is £9.

HOWIE'S *Scottish/Fusion* ££

☎ 556 5766; www.howies.uk.com; 29 Waterloo Pl; ⏰ noon-2.30pm & 5.30-10pm; 🚌 1, 5, 7, 14, 19, 22, 25, 34 or 49; Ⓥ ♿

A bright and airy Georgian corner house provides the elegant setting

NEIGHBOURHOODS

NEW TOWN

V

The long-established and still popular Henderson's Salad Table (p85)

for this, the most central of Howie's four hugely popular Edinburgh restaurants. Their recipe for success includes fresh Scottish produce simply prepared, good-value, seasonally changing menus and eminently quaffable house wines from £12 a bottle.

🍴 LA P'TITE FOLIE French   ££
☎ 225 7983; www.laptitefolie.co.uk; 61 Frederick St; ◷ noon-3pm & 6-11pm Mon-Sat, 6-11pm Sun; 🚌 13, 24, 29 or 42
Breton-owned La P'tite Folie is a delightful little wood-panelled bistro where the menu takes in the French classics – *moules marinières* (mussels) and *coq au vin* (chicken casserole with red wine and mushrooms) – as well as steaks, seafood

and a range of *plats du jour*. The two-course lunch is a bargain at £9. There's another branch in the West End (p103).

🍴 L'ARTICHAUT
Vegetarian   ££
☎ 558 1608; www.lartichaut.co.uk; 14 Eyre Pl; ◷ noon-2.30pm & 6-9pm Tue-Sat, 12.30-8pm Sun; 🚌 113, 17 or 36
Beautifully crafted Tim Stead tables and chairs reflect the care and craftsmanship that goes into the food at this new and inventive restaurant. Fresh, seasonal produce is used to create dishes such as rosemary and thyme pancake filled with aubergine and mozzarella, and spicy black bean stew with glazed chicory and spiced cauliflower.

🍽 LOCANDA DE GUSTI

Italian ££

☎ 558 9581; 7-11 East London St;
🕐 5-11pm Mon, noon-2.30pm & 5-11pm
Tue-Fri, noon-11pm Sat, 10.30am-10pm
Sun; 🚌 8 or 17

This bustling bistro, loud with the buzz of conversation and the clink of glasses and cutlery, is no ordinary Italian, but a little corner of cosmopolitan Naples complete with hearty Neapolitan home cooking by friendly head chef Rosario. The food ranges from light and tasty *pasta fresca* (ravioli tossed with butter and sage) to delicious platters of grilled langoustine, sea bream and sea bass.

🍽 MUSSEL INN *Seafood* ££

☎ 225 5979; www.mussel-inn.com; 61-65 Rose St; 🕐 noon-3pm & 5.30-10pm
Mon-Thu, noon-10pm Fri-Sun; 🚌 all
Princes St buses; ♿

Owned by shellfish farmers, the Mussel Inn provides a direct outlet for fresh Scottish seafood. A busy, informal restaurant decorated with beech furniture, its tables spill out onto the pavement in summer. A kilogram pot of mussels with a choice of sauces – try leek, Dijon mustard and cream – costs £11.50.

🍽 NUMBER ONE *Scottish* £££

☎ 557 6727; www.restaurantnumber
one.com; Balmoral Hotel, 1 Princes St;
🕐 6.30-10pm; 🚌 3, 8, 25, 31 or 33

This is the stylish and sophisticated chatelaine of Edinburgh's city-centre restaurants, all gold-and-velvet elegance with a Michelin star sparkling on her crown. The food is top-notch modern Scottish (choose from a three-course dinner for £59, or a six-course tasting menu for £65) and the service is just on the right side of fawning.

🍽 OLOROSO

Modern Scottish £££

☎ 226 7614; www.oloroso.co.uk;
33 Castle St; 🕐 noon-2.30pm & 7-10.30pm; 🚌 13, 19, 37 or 41

Oloroso is one of Edinburgh's sexiest restaurants, perched on a glass-encased New Town rooftop with views across a Mary Poppins chimneyscape to the Firth of Forth. Swathed in cream linen and charcoal upholstery enlivened with splashes of deep yellow, the dining room serves top-notch Scottish produce with Asian and Mediterranean touches. On a fine afternoon you can savour a snack and a drink on the outdoor roof terrace while soaking up the sun and a view of the castle.

🍽 STAC POLLY *Scottish* £££

☎ 556 2231; www.stacpolly.com; 29-33
Dublin St; 🕐 noon-2.30pm & 6-11pm
Mon-Fri, 6-11pm Sat; 🚌 10, 11, 16 or 17

Named after a mountain in northwestern Scotland, Stac

Polly's kitchen adds sophisticated twists to fresh Highland produce. The dining room, a cosy maze of stone-walled cellars, is formal but intimate, and dishes such as loin of venison with redcurrant and rosemary jus, or baked halibut with sorrel and asparagus, keep the punters coming back for more.

THE DOGS
British   £-££
☎ 220 1208; www.thedogsonline.co.uk; 110 Hanover St; ☾ noon-4pm & 5-10pm; 🚌 13, 23 or 27

Currently one of the coolest tables in town, this bistro-style place uses cheaper cuts of meat and less well-known, more sustainable species of fish to create hearty, no-nonsense dishes such as lamb sweetbreads on toast, and baked coley with *skirlie* (fried oatmeal and onion).

URBAN ANGEL *Bistro*   ££
☎ 225 6215; www.urban-angel.co.uk; 121 Hanover St; ☾ 9am-10pm Mon-Sat, 10am-5pm Sun; 🚌 13, 23 or 27

A wholesome deli that puts the emphasis on Fairtrade, organic and locally sourced produce, Urban Angel also has a delightfully informal cafe-bistro that serves all-day brunch (porridge with honey, French toast with maple syrup, eggs Benedict), tapas, and a wide range of light, snacky meals such as spiced organic lamb meat-balls with fresh coriander mash.

VALVONA & CROLLA CAFFÈ BAR *Italian/Cafe*   ££
☎ 556 6066; www.valvonacrolla.com; 19 Elm Row; ☾ 8.30am-5.30pm Mon-Thu, 8am-6pm Fri & Sat, 10.30am-3.30pm Sun; 🚌 all Leith Walk buses; 📶

The menu at this bright and cheerful cafe, tucked away at the back of the famous deli (p82), is based on family recipes from central and southern Italy, such as *rigatoni all'amatriciana* (pasta with Italian smoked bacon and tomato sauce) and *frittata con fava* (omelette made with broad beans, fresh herbs and Parmigiano Reggiano). Fancy some wine with that? Choose a bottle from the deli on your way in and have it served at your table (£6 corkage).

VALVONA & CROLLA VINCAFFÈ *Italian*   £££
☎ 557 0088; www.valvonacrolla.co.uk; 11 Multrees Walk, St Andrew Sq; ☾ 9.30am-late Mon-Sat, noon-5pm Sun; 🚌 all St Andrew Sq buses; 🅥

Foodie colours dominate at this delightful Italian bistro: bottle-green pillars and banquettes, chocolate- and cream-coloured walls, espresso-black tables. The food is straightforward but made with the finest-quality ingredients,

NEIGHBOURHOODS

NEW TOWN

from superb antipasto to *taglierini con chanterelle* (egg pasta with chanterelle mushrooms sauteed with garlic and chilli and topped with Parmigiano Reggiano).

DRINK

☿ ABBOTSFORD Pub

☎ 225 5276; 3 Rose St; ☼ 11am-11pm Mon-Sat; ☒ all Princes St buses

Dating from 1902 and named after Sir Walter Scott's country house, the Abbotsford is one of the few pubs in Rose St that has retained its Edwardian splendour, with a grand mahogany island bar. It has long been a hang-out for writers, actors, journalists and media people and has many loyal regulars.

☿ AMICUS APPLE Cocktail Bar

☎ 226 6055; www.amicusapple.com; 15 Frederick St; ☼ 10am-1am; ☒ all Princes St buses

Cream leather sofas and dark brown armchairs, bold design and funky lighting make this laid-back cocktail lounge the hippest hang-out in the New Town. The drinks menu ranges from retro classics, such as Bloody Mary and mojito, to original and unusual concoctions such as the Cuillin Martini (Tanqueray No 10 gin, Talisker malt whisky and smoked rosemary).

☿ BASEMENT Bar

☎ 557 0097; www.thebasement.org.uk; 10a-12a Broughton St; ☼ noon-1am; ☒ 8 or 17

The Basement is a laid-back and pleasantly grungy bar – check out the weird, welded furniture made from tank-tracks, camshafts and motorcycle chains – with staff decked out in Hawaiian shirts that are almost as loud as the decor. Background tunes are upbeat but

Rest your beer on a cask or a barrel at the convivial Cask & Barrel (p90)

not intrusive and, if you get peckish, excellent Mediterranean and Mexican munchies are available.

☎ BRAMBLE *Cocktail Bar*
☎ 226 6343; www.bramblebar.co.uk; 16a Queen St; ⏱ 4pm-1am; 🚌 13, 23 or 27
One of those places that easily earns the sobriquet 'best kept secret', Bramble is an unmarked cellar bar where a maze of stone and brick hideaways conceals what is arguably the city's best cocktail bar. No beer taps, no fuss, just expertly mixed drinks.

☎ CAFÉ ROYAL CIRCLE BAR *Pub*
☎ 556 1884; 17 W Register St; ⏱ 11am-11pm Mon-Wed, 11am-midnight Thu, 11am-1am Fri & Sat, 12.30-11pm Sun; 🚌 all Princes St buses
Perhaps *the* classic Edinburgh bar, the Café Royal's main claims to fame are its magnificent oval bar and the series of Doulton tile portraits of famous Victorian inventors. Check out the bottles on the gantry – staff line them up so it looks as if there's a mirror there, and many a drink-befuddled customer has been seen squinting and wondering why they can't see their reflection.

☎ CASK & BARREL *Pub*
☎ 556 3132; 115 Broughton St; ⏱ 11am-1am; 🚌 8 or 17

At the foot of Broughton St, the spit-and-sawdust style Cask & Barrel is a beer-drinker's delight, with a selection of up to 10 real ales, as well as Czech and German beers, and a more than adequate array of TV screens for keeping up with the football or rugby.

☎ CLARK'S BAR *Pub*
☎ 556 1067; 142 Dundas St; ⏱ 11am-11pm Mon-Wed, 11am-11.30pm Thu-Sat, 12.30-11pm Sun; 🚌 23 or 27
A century old and still going strong, Clark's caters to a clientele of real-ale aficionados, football fans (there are three TVs), local office workers and loyal regulars, who appreciate an old-fashioned, no-frills pub with lots of wood panelling and polished brass, and cosy little back rooms for convivial storytelling.

☎ CUMBERLAND BAR *Pub*
☎ 558 3134; 1-3 Cumberland St; ⏱ 11am-1am Mon-Sat, 12.30pm-1am Sun; 🚌 13
Immortalised as the stereotypical New Town pub in Alexander McCall Smith's serialised novel *44 Scotland Street*, the Cumberland has an authentic, traditional wood-brass-and-mirrors look (despite it being relatively modern), and it serves well-looked-after, cask-conditioned ales as well as a wide range of malt whiskies. There's also a pleasant little beer garden outside.

☑ ELBOW *Bar*
☎ 556 5662; www.elbowedinburgh
.co.uk; 133-135 E Claremont St; ☷ 11am-
1am; 🚌 13

An attractive mix of modern and retro style makes Elbow one of the New Town's most appealing neighbourhood bars, with staff who make you feel welcome, a tempting menu of wines and cocktails, and regular pub quizzes and live music nights.

☑ GUILDFORD ARMS *Pub*
☎ 556 4312; 1 W Register St; ☷ 11am-
11pm Mon-Thu, 11am-midnight Fri & Sat,
12.30pm-midnight Sun; 🚌 all Princes
St buses

Located next door to the Café Royal (p90), the Guildford is another classic Victorian pub full of polished mahogany, brass and ornate cornices. The beer is excellent and the bar lunches are good; try to get a table in the unusual upstairs gallery, with a view over the sea of drinkers down below.

☑ JOSEPH PEARCE'S *Pub*
☎ 556 4140; www.bodabar.com; 23 Elm
Row; ☷ 11am-midnight; 🚌 all Leith
Walk buses

A traditional Victorian pub that has been remodeled and given a new lease of life by Swedish owners, Pearce's has become a real hub of the local community, with good food (very family friendly before 5pm), a relaxed atmosphere, and events like Monday night Scrabble games and summer crayfish parties.

☑ KAY'S BAR *Pub*
☎ 225 1858; 39 Jamaica St; ☷ 11am-
midnight Mon-Thu, 11am-1am Fri & Sat,
12.30-11pm Sun; 🚌 13, 24, 29 or 42

Housed in a former wine-merchant's office, tiny Kay's Bar is a cosy haven with red leather benches, a gleaming mahogany bar and a fine range of real ales and malt whiskies. Old wine and sherry barrels adorn one wall, and a cast-iron fireplace holds a coal fire in winter. At lunchtime food is served in the tiny back room (only two tables, so get in early or book ahead).

☑ KENILWORTH *Pub*
☎ 226 4385; 152-154 Rose St;
☷ 9.30am-11pm Mon-Thu, 9.30am-
12.45am Fri & Sat, 12.30-11pm Sun;
🚌 all Princes St buses

A gorgeous Edwardian drinking palace, complete with original fittings – from the tile floors, mahogany circle bar and gantry, to the ornate mirrors and gas lamps – the Kenilworth was Edinburgh's original gay bar back in the 1970s. Today it attracts a mixed crowd of all ages and serves a good range of real ales and malt whiskies.

☕ MATHERS Pub

☎ 556 6754; 25 Broughton St; ⏰ 11am-midnight Mon-Thu, 11am-12.30am Fri & Sat, 12.30-11pm Sun; 🚌 8 or 17

Mathers is the 40-something generation's equivalent of the 20-something's Basement bar (p89) across the street: a friendly, relaxed pub with Edwardian decor serving real ales and good pub grub, with football and rugby matches on the TV.

☕ OLOROSO LOUNGE BAR Cocktail Bar

☎ 226 7614; www.oloroso.co.uk; 33 Castle St; ⏰ 11am-1am Mon-Sat, 12.30pm-1am Sun; 🚌 13, 19, 37 or 41

The rooftop lounge at the Oloroso restaurant (p87) would be at home in New York, Paris or London. Sleek leather sofas and floor-to-ceiling windows allow views across the city to Arthur's Seat, and gourmet drinks include the Berry Balsamic Champagne Cocktail (Pommery rosé blended with strawberries, black pepper and balsamic vinegar).

☕ OXFORD BAR Pub

☎ 539 7119; www.oxfordbar.com; 8 Young St; ⏰ 11am-1am Mon-Sat, 12.30pm-1am Sun; 🚌 13, 19, 37 or 41

The Oxford is that rarest of things these days, a real pub for real people, with no theme, no music, no frills and no pretensions. The 'Ox' has been immortalised by Ian Rankin, author of the Inspector Rebus novels, who is a regular here, as is his fictional detective.

☕ REGENT Pub

☎ 661 8198; 2 Montrose Tce; ⏰ 11am-1am Mon-Sat, 12.30pm-1am Sun; 🚌 15 or 35

This is a pleasant, gay local with a relaxed atmosphere (no loud music), serving coffee and croissants plus excellent real ales, including Deuchars IPA and Caledonian 80/-. Meeting place for the Lesbian and Gay Real Ale Drinkers club (9pm first Monday of the month).

☕ ROBERTSONS 37 Pub

☎ 225 6185; 37 Rose St; ⏰ 11am-11pm Mon-Sat; 🚌 all Princes St buses

No 37 is to malt whisky connoisseurs what the Diggers once was to real-ale fans. Its long gantry sports a choice of more than 100 single malts, and the bar provides a quiet and elegant environment in which to sample them.

☕ TIGERLILY Cocktail Bar

☎ 225 5005; www.tigerlilyedinburgh .co.uk; 125 George St; ⏰ 11am-1am; 🚌 all Princes St buses

Swirling textured wallpapers, glittering chain-mail curtains, crystal chandeliers and plush pink and gold sofas have won a cluster of design awards for this boutique hotel bar, where sharp suits and stiletto heels line the banquettes. There's expertly mixed cocktails, as well as Japanese Kirin beer on draught and Innis & Gunn Scottish ale in bottles.

▼ TONIC *Cocktail Bar*
☎ 225 6431; www.bar-tonic.co.uk; 34a N Castle St; ⊗ noon-1am; 🚍 13, 24, 29 or 42

As cool and classy as a perfectly mixed martini, Tonic prides itself on the quality and authenticity of its cocktails, of which there are more than a hundred to choose from. The bar's cream and burgundy decor includes polished wood and limestone, and the clientele ranges from local office workers on work-a-day lunch breaks to celebrities visiting the Edinburgh International Festival.

PLAY

❖ CC BLOOMS *Club*
☎ 556 9331; www.bebo.com/ccblooms nightclub; 23 Greenside Pl; ⊗ 6pm-3am Mon-Sat, 7pm-3am Sun; 🚍 all Leith St buses

The long-reigning queen of the Edinburgh gay scene, CC's offers two floors of deafening dance and disco. It's a bit overpriced and often overcrowded but still worth a visit – if you can get past the bouncers. Go early, or sample

the wild karaoke on Thursday and Sunday nights.

❖ EDINBURGH PLAYHOUSE *Theatre*
☎ 524 3301, bookings 0870 606 3424; www.edinburgh-playhouse.co.uk; 18-22 Greenside Pl; tickets £10-30; ⊗ box office 10am-6pm Mon-Sat, to 8pm on show nights; 🚍 all Leith Walk buses

This restored theatre at the top of Leith Walk stages Broadway musicals, dance shows, opera and popular-music concerts.

❖ JAM HOUSE *Live Music*
☎ 226 4380; www.thejamhouse.com; 5 Queen St; admission free before 8pm, £6 after; ⊗ 6pm-3am Fri & Sat; 🚍 all York Pl buses

The brainchild of rhythm'n'blues pianist and TV personality Jools Holland, the Jam House is set in a former BBC TV studio and offers a combination of fine dining and live jazz and blues performances. Admission is for over-21s only, and there's a smart-casual dress code.

❖ LULU *Club*
☎ 225 5005; www.luluedinburgh .co.uk; 125 George St; admission free-£10; ⊗ 8pm-3am Thu-Sun; 🚍 all Princes St buses

Lush leather sofas, red satin cushions, fetishistic steel mesh curtains and dim red lighting all help to

Philip Ritchie
Youth development worker and Highland dancer

You're a Highland dancer? Yes, I've been dancing since I was four years old, and competed in national championships till I was 17. I still perform at tourist shows such as Jamie's Scottish Evening at the King James Hotel. **Where would you recommend for a taste of traditional Scottish music and dance?** There are summer performances at the Ross Bandstand in Princes Street Gardens (p77) – check www.princesstreetgardensdancing.org.uk for dates – but if you want to join in, check out the Friday night ceilidhs at Ghillie Dhu (p105). The Ghillie also has live music on Saturdays, but for more down-to-earth folk music sessions you can't beat Sandy Bell's (p63). If you want to take lessons, the New Scotland Country Dance Society (www.newscotland.org.uk) runs classes. **And a good place to stretch your legs before a jig?** The Royal Botanic Garden (p98) – great views of the city skyline, and the festival fireworks too.

create a decadent atmosphere in this drop-dead-gorgeous club venue beneath the Tigerlily boutique hotel. Resident and guest DJs show a bit more originality than at your average club.

⭐ OPAL LOUNGE *Cocktail Bar*
☎ 226 2275; www.opallounge.co.uk; 51 George St; ☽ noon-3am; 🚌 24, 41 or 42

One of Edinburgh's trendiest bars, the Opal is jammed at weekends with affluent 20-somethings who've spent two hours in front of the mirror achieving that artlessly scruffy look. During the week, when the air-kissing, cocktail-sipping crowds thin out, it's a good place to relax with a fruit smoothie (or one of those expensive but excellent cocktails) and sample the tasty Asian food on offer.

⭐ STAND COMEDY CLUB
Comedy
☎ 558 7272; www.thestand.co.uk; 5 York Pl; admission free-£15; 🚌 all York Pl buses

The Stand, founded in 1995, is Edinburgh's main comedy venue. It's a cabaret bar – you can eat and drink as well as laugh – with shows every night (doors open 7.30pm),

plenty of big-name appearances, and a free improv show at Sunday lunchtime.

⭐ VOODOO ROOMS
Club/Live Music
☎ 556 7060; www.thevoodoorooms .com; 19a West Register St; admission free-£10; ☽ noon-1am Fri-Sun, 4pm-1am Mon-Thu; 🚌 all Princes St buses

Decadent decor of black leather, ornate plasterwork and gilt detailing create a funky setting for this complex of bars and performance spaces above the Café Royal that host everything from classic soul and Motown to Vegas lounge club nights (www.vegasscotland.co.uk) to live local bands.

⭐ VUE CINEMA
Cinema
☎ 0871-224 0240; Omni Centre, Greenside Pl; tickets £7.80; 🚌 all Leith Walk buses

A 12-screen multiplex cinema, with three 'VIP' screens (tickets £9.20) where you can watch your movie of choice from the comfort of a luxurious leather reclining seat complete with side table for your drink and complimentary snacks.

>WEST END & STOCKBRIDGE

This neighbourhood stretches from the western edge of the New Town south to Lothian Rd, west to Haymarket and north to Stockbridge, taking in the new financial district called the Exchange, the shopping streets of the West End, and Haymarket, home to Edinburgh's other train station. There are few tourist attractions here, but you'll find some good places to stay and some excellent places to eat.

The Georgian terraces of the New Town extend into the West End, Edinburgh's 'diplomatic quarter', dotted with foreign consulates and upmarket hotels. The new Exchange district to its south is a maze of chrome, glass and sandstone modernity, with people in suits striding purposefully between office blocks. This area is now the city's financial powerhouse, home to many banks and insurance-company head-quarters. Stockbridge, originally a mill village, is a bohemian enclave of neighbourhood bistros, posh pubs and some interesting jewellery shops.

WEST END & STOCKBRIDGE

◉ SEE
Dean Gallery 1 C3
Royal Botanic Garden 2 E1
Scottish National
   Gallery of Modern Art ..3 C3

🏠 SHOP
Adam Pottery 4 E2
Annie Smith 5 D2
Arkangel 6 D3
Bliss 7 D2
Edinburgh Farmers
   Market 8 E4
Galerie Mirages 9 D2
Helen Bateman 10 D4
Ian Mellis 11 E2
Kiss the Fish 12 D2
McAlister Matheson
   Music 13 E4

Ocean 14 E4
Sam Thomas 15 D3
Second Edition 16 F1
Wonderland 17 E4

🍴 EAT
Blue ....(see 40)
Buffalo Grill 18 E2
Cafe Newton ....(see 1)
Channings Restaurant ..19 D2
Chop Chop 20 D4
Escargot Blanc 21 D3
La P'tite Folie 22 E3
New Edinburgh
   Rendezvous 23 E3
Omar Khayyam 24 D4
Rainbow Arch 25 E4
Songkran 26 D3
Songkran II 27 E2

🍸 DRINK
Antiquary 28 E2
Avoca Bar 29 D2
Bailie Bar 30 E2
Bert's Bar 31 D3
Ghillie Dhu 32 E3
Indigo Yard 33 E3
Sygn 34 E3

★ PLAY
Filmhouse 35 E4
Glenogle Swim
   Centre 36 E1
One Spa 37 E4
Royal Lyceum
   Theatre 38 E4
Skindulgence Spa 39 E2
Traverse Theatre 40 E4
Usher Hall 41 E4

NEIGHBOURHOODS

WEST END & STOCKBRIDGE

SEE

DEAN GALLERY

☎ 624 6200; www.nationalgalleries .org; 73 Belford Rd; admission free, fee for special exhibitions; 🕙 10am-5pm daily, noon-5pm 1 Jan, closed 25 & 26 Dec; 🚌 13; 🕭

An imposing neoclassical mansion topped with monumental towers, the Dean holds the Gallery of Modern Art's collection of Dada and surrealist art, including works by Dali, Giacometti and Picasso, and a large collection of sculpture and graphic art created by the Edinburgh-born sculptor Sir Eduardo Paolozzi. A smaller version of Paolozzi's statue of Newton (which stands outside the British Library in London) is in the garden.

ROYAL BOTANIC GARDEN

☎ 552 7171; www.rbge.org.uk; 20a Inverleith Row; admission free; 🕙 10am-7pm Apr-Sep, 10am-6pm Mar & Oct, 10am-4pm Nov-Feb; 🚌 8, 17, 23, 27 or 37

Originally founded near Holyrood in 1670 and moved to its present location in 1823, Edinburgh's Botanic Garden is the second-oldest institution of its kind in Britain (after the garden in Oxford), and one of the most respected in the world. Seventy beautifully landscaped acres include splendid Victorian palm houses, colourful swathes of rhododendron and azalea, and a world-famous rock garden. The garden's Terrace Café offers good views towards the city centre.

SCOTTISH NATIONAL GALLERY OF MODERN ART

☎ 624 6200; www.nationalgalleries .org; 75 Belford Rd; admission free, fee for special exhibitions; 🕙 10am-5pm daily, noon-5pm 1 Jan, closed 25 & 26 Dec; 🚌 13; 🕭

Housed in bright, modern exhibition rooms that belie the building's austere neoclassical facade, the Scottish National Gallery of Modern

EDINBURGH ZOO

Opened in 1913, **Edinburgh Zoo** (☎ 334 9171; www.edinburghzoo.org.uk; 134 Corstorphine Rd; adult/child £10.50/7.50; 🕙 9am-6pm Apr-Sep, 9am-5pm Oct & Mar, 9am-4.30pm Nov-Feb; 🚌 12, 26, 31 or 100; 🕭) is one of the world's leading conservation zoos. Its captive breeding programme has saved many endangered species, including Siberian tigers, pygmy hippos and red pandas. The main attractions are the penguins (kept in the world's biggest penguin pool), the sea lion and red panda feeding times (check website for details), the animal-handling sessions and the Lifelinks 'hands-on' zoology centre. The zoo is 2.5 miles west of the city centre.

WATER OF LEITH

Edinburgh's river is a modest stream, flowing only 20 miles from the northwestern slopes of the Pentland Hills to enter the Firth of Forth at Leith. It cuts a surprisingly rural swathe through the city, providing an important wildlife habitat (you can occasionally see otters and kingfishers) and offering the chance to stroll along wooded riverbanks only 500m from Princes St. The Water of Leith Walkway offers an almost uninterrupted 12-mile walking and cycling route along the river from Leith to the village of Balerno, on the southwestern edge of the city.

The **Water of Leith Visitor Centre** (☎ 455 7367; www.waterofleith.org.uk; 24 Lanark Rd; admission free; ☻ 10am-4pm, closed 24 Dec-3 Jan; 🚍 28, 35, 44 or 66; 🚻) has interactive displays on the river's wildlife and ecology, and underwater video cameras providing live images of aquatic creatures.

Art concentrates on 20th-century art, with various European art movements represented by the likes of Matisse, Picasso, Kokoschka, Magritte, Miro, Mondrian and Giacometti. American and English artists are also represented, but most space is given to Scottish painters – from the Scottish Colourists of the early 20th century to contemporary artists such as Peter Howson and Ken Currie. The post-Impressionist works of the Scottish Colourists (Peploe, Hunter, Caddell and Fergusson) are especially popular; in *Reflections, Balloch*, Hunter pulls off the improbable trick of making Scotland look like the south of France. Stairs behind the gallery lead down to the Water of Leith Walkway, where you can find *6 Times* by Anthony Gormley, consisting of six human figures standing at various points along the river.

 SHOP

🛍 **ADAM POTTERY** *Arts & Crafts*

☎ 557 3978; www.adampottery.co.uk; 76 Henderson Row; ☻ 10am-5.30pm Mon-Sat; 🚍 36

This small independent pottery produces its own colourfully glazed ceramics, both decorative and functional, in a wide range of styles, with objects ranging from coffee cups to garden planters. Visitors are welcome to watch potters at work in the studio.

🛍 **ANNIE SMITH** *Jewellery*

☎ 332 5749; 20 Raeburn Pl; www.annie smith.co.uk; ☻ 10am-5.30pm Mon-Sat, noon-5pm Sun; 🚍 24, 29 or 42

Annie Smith's back-of-the-shop studio creates beautiful and original contemporary jewellery in silver and 18-carat gold, with beaten and worked surfaces that reflect natural textures such as

WEST END & STOCKBRIDGE

rock, ice and leaves. If there's nothing in the shop that takes your fancy, you can commission Ms Smith to make something to order.

☐ ARKANGEL *Fashion*
☎ 226 4466; www.arkangelfashion .co.uk; 4 William St; ⏱ 10am-5.30pm Mon-Wed, Fri & Sat, 10am-6.30pm Thu; ☒ all Shandwick Pl buses
Owners Janey and Lulu will help you pick out a glamorous outfit from their carefully selected wardrobe of off-beat European chic and vintage fashion – look out for designer wear by Antoine & Lilli and Irene Van Ryb, and jewellery by Angela Caputi and Martine Boissy.

☐ BLISS *Gifts*
☎ 332 4605; 5 Raeburn Pl; ⏱ 10am-5.30pm Mon-Sat, 1-5pm Sun; ☒ 24, 29 or 42
This is a great place for girly gifts, from colourful handmade cards and giftwrap to copper and silver jewellery, scented candles, art prints and accessories.

☐ EDINBURGH FARMERS MARKET *Food & Drink*
☎ 652 5940; www.edinburghfarmers market.com; Castle Tce; ⏱ 9am-2pm Sat; ☒ 28
This colourful weekly event attracts stallholders who sell everything from wild boar, venison and home-cured pedigree bacon to organic bread, free-range eggs, honey and handmade soap.

☐ GALERIE MIRAGES *Gifts*
☎ 315 2603; 46a Raeburn Pl; www .galeriemirages.co.uk; ⏱ 10am-5.30pm Mon-Sat, 1-5pm Sun; ☒ 24, 29 or 42
A narrow lane between two houses leads to this Aladdin's Cave packed with jewellery, textiles and handicrafts from all over the world. It's best known for its silver, amber and gemstone jewellery in both ethnic and contemporary designs, but you'll also find things like scented sandalwood boxes, handmade paper goods, colourful cushions and gorgeous throws.

☐ HELEN BATEMAN *Shoes*
☎ 220 4495; www.helenbateman.com; 16 William St; ⏱ 9.30am-6pm Mon-Sat; ☒ all Shandwick Pl buses
From sparkly stilettos and sleek satin pumps to 1950s-style open-sided court shoes and soft suede loafers, Helen Bateman's shop has every kind of handmade shoe and boot you could wish for. You can even order customised satin shoes – slingbacks, pumps or kitten heels – dyed to any colour and decorated with whatever your heart desires.

⊡ IAN MELLIS *Food & Drink*
☎ 225 6566; www.mellischeese.co.uk; 6 Bakers Pl, Kerr St; ⏱ 9.30am-6pm Mon-Wed, 9.30am-6.30pm Thu, 9.30am-7pm Fri, 9am-6pm Sat, 11am-5pm Sun; 🚍 24, 29 or 42

Branch of the famous Old Town cheese shop (p51).

⊡ KISS THE FISH *Gifts*
☎ 332 8912; www.kissthefishstudios.com; 9 Dean Park St; ⏱ 10am-5.30pm Mon-Sat, 11am-4.30pm Sun; 🚍 24, 29 or 42; ♿

This is not just a gift shop, but also an arts and crafts studio where kids can get their hands on stuff to make and decorate.

⊡ MCALISTER MATHESON MUSIC *Music*
☎ 228 3827; www.mmmusic.co.uk; 1 Grindlay St; ⏱ 9.30am-6pm Mon-Thu, 9.30am-6.30pm Fri, 9am-5.30pm Sat; 🚍 2 or 35

This is Scotland's biggest and most knowledgeable shop for classical music CDs, DVDs and books – just about every staff member seems to have a music degree. It also stocks a selection of Scottish folk and Celtic music.

⊡ OCEAN *Jewellery*
☎ 229 6767; www.oceanjewellery.co.uk; 39 Lothian Rd; ⏱ 10am-5.45pm Mon-Fri, 10am-5.30pm Sat, noon-4pm Sun; 🚍 all Lothian Rd buses

Sells a fantastic range of jewellery in contemporary designs by top Scottish and international designers, including silver, gemstones and pearls. Also watches by Steel and Opex, and handbags by matt & nat.

⊡ SAM THOMAS *Fashion*
☎ 226 1126; 18 Stafford St; www.sam-thomas.co.uk; ⏱ 9.30am-6pm Mon-Sat; 🚍 all Shandwick Pl buses

With the entrance on William St, this place has a range of affordable designer gear, from casual to evening wear, as well as reasonably priced accessories, including jewellery, bags, belts, boots and shoes.

⊡ SECOND EDITION *Books*
☎ 556 9403; 9 Howard St; ⏱ 10am-5.30pm Tue-Sat; 🚍 8, 17, 23 or 27

This is a small bookshop for serious collectors buying and selling rare editions, with a good range of titles on Scottish subjects. The owner often goes to buy books on weekday mornings, so wait until after noon if you want to be absolutely sure that the shop will be open.

⊡ WONDERLAND *Toys*
☎ 229 6428; www.wonderlandmodels.com; 97-101 Lothian Rd; ⏱ 9.30am-6pm Mon-Fri, 9am-6pm Sat; 🚍 all Lothian Rd buses

Wonderland is a classic kids-with-their-noses-pressed-against-the-window toy shop that is filled

The Water of Leith (p99) adds a rural touch to the city

with model aircraft, spaceships and radio-controlled cars and all sorts of other desirable things, but it also caters to the serious train set and model-making fraternity.

 # EAT

BLUE *Scottish* ££
☎ 221 1222; www.bluescotland.co.uk; 10 Cambridge St; ☽ noon-2.30pm & 5.30-10.30pm Mon-Thu, to 11pm Fri & Sat; 🚌 all Lothian Rd buses

Set above the foyer of the Traverse Theatre (p107), this is a cool white minimalist space with polished oak and Danish designer furniture. The food is simple but skilfully cooked and presented. Choices include Crombie's sausages with mash and onion gravy,

and ribeye steak with bearnaise and chunky chips. Two courses costs £16 between 5.30pm and 7.30pm.

BUFFALO GRILL
American ££-£££
☎ 332 3864; www.buffalogrill.co.uk; 1 Raeburn Pl; ☽ 6-10.30pm Mon-Thu, 6-11pm Fri, 5-11pm Sat, 5-10.30pm Sun; 🚌 24, 32 or 49

This Stockbridge incarnation of Buffalo Grill is a bit more spacious than the original branch (p117), but has the same Wild West decor and beefy, all-American menu. Unlike the original branch this place is fully licensed, but they still allow you to BYOB if you prefer (£1 corkage per bottle of wine).

CAFE NEWTON *Cafe* £
☎ 624 6273; 72 Belford Rd; ⏱ 10am-4.30pm; 🚌 13

The elegant cafe in the Dean Gallery (p98) is decked out in smart black and white decor, dominated by a gleaming Victoria Arduino espresso machine and a plaster model of Eduardo Paolozzi's statue of Isaac Newton. As well as temtping coffee and cake, the Mediterranean-influenced lunch menu (noon to 2.30pm) offers tasty homemade soups and platters of antipasti, foccaccia filled with smoked chicken, roast peppers etc.

CHANNINGS RESTAURANT *Scottish/Mediterranean* ££
☎ 315 2225; www.channings.co.uk; 12-16 South Learmonth Gardens; ⏱ noon-2.30pm & 6-10pm Mon-Sat, 12.30-3pm & 6-10pm Sun; 🚌 19, 37 or 41

The restaurant at Channings Hotel is a relaxing modern space, bright and lively at lunchtime, low-lit and intimate in the evening. The menu offers fresh Scottish produce served with a Mediterranean twist, such as leek and mascarpone risotto with a poached free range egg.

CHOP CHOP *Chinese* ££
☎ 221 1155; www.chop-chop.co.uk; 248 Morrison St; ⏱ noon-2pm & 5.30-10pm; 🚌 all Haymarket buses

Chop Chop is a Chinese restaurant with a difference, serving dishes popular in China rather than Britain; as their slogan says, 'Can a billion people be wrong?'. No sweet and sour pork here, but a range of delicious dumplings filled with pork and coriander, beef and chilli, or lamb and leek, and unusual vegetarian dishes such as aubergine fried with garlic and Chinese spices.

ESCARGOT BLANC *French* ££
☎ 226 1890; www.lescargotblanc.co.uk; 17 Queensferry St; ⏱ noon-3pm & 5.30-10pm Mon-Thu, noon-3pm & 5.30-10.30pm Fri & Sat; 🚌 13, 19, 36, 37 or 41

This superb neighbourhood bistro, with French chef and waitstaff, and two-thirds of its top quality produce sourced in Scotland (one-third imported from France), is a true 'Auld Alliance' of culinary cultures. Choose from a menu of classics such as escargots in garlic, parsley and hazelnut butter, *coq au vin* (made with free-range Scottish chicken), and perfectly prepared Scottish ribeye steak with *bleu d'Auvergne* sauce.

LA P'TITE FOLIE *French* ££
☎ 225 8678; www.laptitefolie.co.uk; 9 Randolph Pl; ⏱ noon-3pm & 6-11pm Mon-Sat; 🚌 13, 19, 37 or 41

Housed in an unusual, Tudor-lookalike building, La P'tite Folie's second branch is completely different in character from the Frederick St original (p86). The upstairs dining room has a pleasantly clubbish feel, with green walls and dark wood – try to grab the table in the little corner turret with its view of the spires of St Mary's Cathedral.

NEW EDINBURGH RENDEZVOUS Chinese ££

☎ 225 2023; www.edinburghrendezvous.co.uk; 10a Queensferry St; 11.45am-11.30pm Mon-Sat, 1-11.30pm Sun; 13, 19, 36, 37 or 41

Edinburgh's oldest Chinese restaurant, dating from 1956, is still one of its best. A no-frills, no-nonsense place, it offers an extensive menu of expertly prepared Cantonese and Peking dishes with classic favourites, such as shredded beef with chilli sauce and aromatic crispy duck, alongside more adventurous dishes, such as shredded sea blubber, boneless duck's feet with mustard sauce, and pickled cabbage with chilli sauce.

OMAR KHAYYAM Indian ££

☎ 220 0024; 1 Grosvenor St; noon-2pm & 5-11pm Mon-Fri, noon-11pm Sat, 4.30-11pm Sun; all Haymarket buses

This is a modern Punjabi restaurant with attentive, waistcoated waiters, stylish modern decor and an unusual water feature trickling away in the middle of the dining room. The food is always fresh and flavourful, ranging from old favourites such as chicken tikka masala to more unusual dishes like Kabul chicken (with chick peas, cumin and coriander).

RAINBOW ARCH Chinese ££

☎ 221 1288; www.rainbowarch.co.uk; 8-16 Morrison St; noon-3am Fri-Tue, noon-midnight Wed & Thu; all Lothian Rd buses

It's always a sign of a good Chinese restaurant when you see members of the local Chinese community eating there, and you'll see plenty of them at the Rainbow Arch. The menu is more adventurous than most – look out for deep-fried minced octopus cakes – and even the standard dishes, such as lemon chicken, are a cut above the average Chinese restaurant.

SONGKRAN Thai ££

☎ 225 7889; 24a Stafford St; noon-2.30pm & 5.30-10.30pm Mon-Sat; all West End buses

Be prepared for a squeeze to get into this tiny basement restaurant! The reason for the crush is some of the best Thai food in Edinburgh – try the tender yang (marinated and barbecued beef, chicken or prawn), the crisp and tart orange chicken, or the chilli-loaded warm beef salad. There are two branches: choose here for lunch, and Songkran II (opposite) for dinner.

☷ SONGKRAN II *Thai* ££

☎ 225 4804; 8 Gloucester St; ☽ noon-2.30pm & 6-10.45pm Mon-Sat, 6-10.45pm Sun; ☐ 24, 29 or 42

Songkran II dishes up the same menu of excellent Thai food as the West End branch (opposite), but in the more romantic atmosphere of a 17th-century town house, decorated with Thai paintings, statues and wood-carvings.

☷ DRINK

ANTIQUARY *Pub*

☎ 225 2858; 72-78 St Stephen St; ☽ 11.30am-11pm Mon, 11.30am-12.30am Tue-Wed, 11.30am-1am Thu-Sat, 12.30pm-12.30am Sun; ☐ 24, 29 or 42; ☈

A dark, downstairs den of traditional beersmanship, with bare wooden floorboards and dark wood tables and chairs, the long-established Antiquary has lively open folk-music sessions on Thursday nights at 9pm, when all- comers are welcome to perform.

☷ AVOCA BAR *Pub*

☎ 315 3311; 4-6 Dean St; ☽ 11am-midnight Mon-Thu, 11am-1am Fri & Sat, noon-midnight Sun; ☐ 24, 29 or 42

Tucked away on a Stockbridge side street, this traditional bar combines a warm, welcoming atmosphere with good food and beer.

☷ BAILIE BAR *Pub*

☎ 225 4673; 2 St Stephen St; ☽ 11am-midnight Mon-Thu, 11am-1am Fri & Sat, 12.30-11pm Sun; ☐ 24, 29 or 42

Tucked down in a basement, the Bailie is an old Stockbridge stalwart; a dimly lit, warm and welcoming nook with a large circular island bar, a roaring fire in winter, and TVs screening live football. Serves good coffee as well as real ales and malt whiskies.

☷ BERT'S BAR *Pub*

☎ 225 5748; 29-31 William St; ☽ 11am-11pm Mon-Wed, 11am-1am Thu-Sat; ☐ all Shandwick Pl buses

A classic re-creation of a 1930s-style pub – a welcoming womb with warm wood and leather decor, complete with a jar of pickled eggs on the bar – Bert's is a good place to sample real ale and down-to-earth pub grub such as Scotch pies and bangers and mash. There is a branch in Stockbridge.

☷ GHILLIE DHU *Pub*

☎ 222 9930; www.ghillie-dhu.co.uk; 2 Rutland Pl; ☽ noon-3am; ☐ all Princes St buses

This spectacular new bar, with its huge, chunky beer hall tables, leather sofa booths, and polished black-and-white tile floor makes a grand setting for the live folk music sessions that take place here every night (admission free).

NEIGHBOURHOODS

WEST END & STOCKBRIDGE

☗ INDIGO YARD *Bar*

☎ 220 5603; www.indigoyardedinburgh
.co.uk; 7 Charlotte Lane; ☽ 8.30am-
1am; ➟ 13, 19, 36, 37 or 41

Set around an airy, stone-floored
and glass-roofed courtyard, Indigo
Yard is a fashionable West End
watering hole that has been pat-
ronised by the likes of Liam Gal-
lagher, Pierce Brosnan and Kylie
Minogue. Good food – including
open-air barbecues during the
summer months – just adds to the
attraction.

Wining and dining at Indigo Yard

☗ SYGN *Cocktail Bar*

☎ 225 6060; www.sygn.co.uk; 15
Charlotte Lane; ☽ 10am-1am; ➟ 13,
19, 36, 37 or 41

The plush banquettes and sleek,
polished tables in this sharply
styled bar are just the place to
pose with a passionfruit bellini or
a glass of Pol Roger. The languid
and laid-back atmosphere at this
bar is complemented by cool
tunes and superb cocktails, and
the food menu is surprisingly
good.

⭐ PLAY

▣ FILMHOUSE *Cinema*

☎ box office 228 2688, info 228 2689;
www.filmhousecinema.com; 88 Lothian
Rd; adult/child £6.90/5.20; ➟ all Lothian
Rd buses; ♿

The Filmhouse screens a full
programme of art-house, classic,
foreign and second-run films, with
lots of themes, retrospectives and
70mm screenings. It's the main
venue for the annual International
Film Festival (p24).

▣ GLENOGLE SWIM CENTRE
Health & Fitness

☎ 343 6376; www.edinburghleisure
.co.uk; Glenogle Rd; adult/child £3.90/2;
☽ 7am-10pm Mon-Fri, 6am-6pm Sat &
Sun; ➟ 36

Atmospheric Victorian swimming
baths with a 25m pool, sauna
and gym.

★ ONE SPA *Health & Fitness*
☎ 221 7777; www.one-spa.com;
Sheraton Grand Hotel, 8 Conference Sq, Lothian Rd; per 25min from £40;
☀ **6.30am-10pm Mon-Fri, 7am-9pm Sat & Sun;** 🚌 **all Lothian Rd buses**
This gorgeous rooftop spa offers a wide range of pampering treatments from reflexology and reiki to facials and hot-stone therapy. The setting is unbeatable, with a beautiful oval indoor pool, rooftop hydrotherapy pool, rustic sauna, curvaceous mosaic-tiled 'aroma grotto', and gym. You can book individual treatment sessions or splash out on a half- or full-day package (from £70 to £295).

★ ROYAL LYCEUM THEATRE
Theatre
☎ 248 4848; www.lyceum.org.uk; 30b
Grindlay St; tickets £10-30; ☀ **box office 10am-6pm Mon-Sat, to 8pm on show nights;** 🚌 **all Lothian Rd buses**
A grand Victorian theatre located beside Usher Hall, the Lyceum stages drama, concerts, musicals and ballet.

★ SKINDULGENCE SPA
Health & Fitness
☎ 225 3350; www.thefloatarium
.vpweb.co.uk; 29 NW Circus Pl; float per hr £35; ☀ **9am-8pm Mon-Fri, 9am-7pm Sat, 10am-5pm Sun;** 🚌 **24, 29 or 42**

Escape from the bustle of the city centre in a warm, womb-like flotation tank, or enjoy the many other therapies on offer, including facials, aromatherapy massage, reflexology, shiatsu, reiki and Indian head massage (appointments necessary). There's a sweet-scented shop, too, where you can buy massage oils, incense, candles, homeopathic remedies, CDs and so on.

★ TRAVERSE THEATRE *Theatre*
☎ 228 1404; www.traverse.co.uk; 10
Cambridge St; tickets £6-18; ☀ **box office 10am-6pm Mon, 10am-8pm Tue-Sat, 4-8pm Sun;** 🚌 **all Lothian Rd buses**
The Traverse Theatre is the main focus for new Scottish writing and stages an adventurous programme of contemporary drama and dance. The box office is open on Sunday only if there is a performance that evening.

★ USHER HALL *Music*
☎ 228 1155; www.usherhall.co.uk;
Lothian Rd; tickets £10-30; ☀ **box office 10.30am-5.30pm Mon-Sat, to 8pm on show nights;** 🚌 **all Lothian Rd buses**
Built in 1914 with money donated by the brewery magnate Andrew Usher, the architecturally impressive 2900-seat Usher Hall hosts concerts by the Royal Scottish National Orchestra and performances of popular music.

>SOUTH EDINBURGH

This neighbourhood extends from the southern edge of the Old Town and Holyrood Park, taking in Tollcross and Bruntsfield, the 19th-century tenement districts of Marchmont and Sciennes (pronounced 'sheens') and the elegant villa quarters of Grange and Newington. Away from the main thoroughfares of Dalkeith Rd, Clerk St/S Clerk St/Newington Rd and Causewayside/Mayfield Rd, it's a peaceful residential neighbourhood of smart Victorian tenement flats and spacious garden villas. There's not much to see in the way of tourist attractions here, but there are many good restaurants, pubs and places to stay.

The northern and eastern parts of the neighbourhood, which include Edinburgh University's main campus (centred on George Sq) and Pollock Halls of Residence, has a sizable student population and the bookshops, bars, cafes and good-value restaurants that go along with it. The south-western part, around Grange and Newington, is characterised by garden villas built in the 19th century for Edinburgh's middle and upper classes.

SOUTH EDINBURGH

◉ SEE
Blackford Hill 1 E6
Surgeons' Hall Museums .2 G1
The Meadows 3 F3
Union Canal 4 D2

🛍 SHOP
Backbeat 5 G2
Biketrax 6 D2
Boardwise 7 D1
Courtyard Antiques 8 G3
Greensleeves 9 C5
Hogs Head 10 G3
Kilberry Bagpipes 11 G3
Meadows Pottery 12 G3
Peckham's 13 C4
West Port Books 14 D1
Word Power 15 F2

🍴 EAT
Ann Purna 16 G2
Buffalo Grill 17 F2

Engine Shed 18 G2
First Coast 19 B2
Jasper's 20 C1
Kalpna 21 G2
Katie's Diner 22 D3
Kebab Mahal 23 F1
Leven's 24 D3
McKirdy's Steakhouse ..25 C1
Mosque Kitchen 26 F2
Point Restaurant 27 D1
Roti 28 D2
Suruchi 29 G1
Sushiya 30 B2
Sweet Melindas 31 F3
Thai Lemongrass 32 D3
Zazou 33 A5

🍸 DRINK
Athletic Arms
  (The Diggers) 34 A3
Auld Hoose 35 G2
Bennet's Bar 36 D2

Blue Blazer 37 D1
Brauhaus 38 D2
Caley Sample Room 39 A3
Canny Man's 40 C6
Cloisters 41 D2
Dragonfly 42 E1
Pear Tree House 43 G2
Southsider 44 G2

⭐ PLAY
Cameo 45 D2
Dominion 46 C5
Edinburgh Festival
  Theatre 47 F1
King's Theatre 48 D2
Queen's Hall 49 G3
Royal Commonwealth
  Pool 50 H3
Stereo 51 D1
Wee Red Bar 52 E2

Please see over for map

SEE
BLACKFORD HILL
Charterhall Rd; 🚌 24, 38 or 41
A patch of countryside enclosed by the city's southern suburbs, craggy Blackford Hill (164m) offers pleasant walking and splendid views. The panorama to the north takes in Edinburgh Castle atop its rock, the bristling spine of the Old Town, the monuments on Calton Hill and the 'sleeping lion' of Arthur's Seat.

MEADOWS
Melville Dr; 🚌 5, 24 or 41
This mile-long stretch of lush grass crisscrossed with tree-lined walks was once a shallow lake known as the Borough Loch. Drained in the 1740s and converted into parkland, it's a great place for a picnic or a quiet walk – in springtime its walks lie ankle-deep in drifts of pink cherry blossom, and there are great views of Arthur's Seat.

SURGEONS' HALL MUSEUMS
☎ 527 1649; www.museum.rcsed.ac.uk; 9 Hill Sq; adult/child £5/3; ⏲ noon-4pm Mon-Fri; 🚌 all South Bridge buses
Surgeons' Hall, a grand Ionic temple built in 1832 to house the Royal College of Surgeons of Edinburgh, houses a fascinating trio of museums. The **History of Surgery Museum** takes a look at surgery in Scotland from the 15th century, when barbers supplemented their income with blood-letting, amputations and other surgical procedures, to the body-snatching anatomists of the 18th and 19th centuries. The highlight is an exhibit on Burke and Hare (p152), which includes Burke's death mask and a pocketbook bound in his skin. The **Dental Museum** displays a wince-inducing collection of extraction tools, while the **Pathology Museum** houses a gruesome but compelling 19th-century collection of diseased organs and tumours pickled in formaldehyde.

GILMERTON COVE
The latest addition to Edinburgh's subterranean tourist attractions is **Gilmerton Cove** (☎ 557 6464; www.gilmertoncove.org.uk; 16 Drum St, Gilmerton; guided tours adult/child £5/4; ⏲ tours 10am-7pm Mon-Sat, by appointment only; 🚌 3 or 29), a collection of passages and chambers hewn out of solid sandstone on the southeastern fringes of the city. Its origins are uncertain, but tradition maintains that it was created by a local blacksmith in the early 18th century, and used as a forge, workshop and illegal drinking den. To visit, you have to book a guided tour through Rosslyn Tours (www.rosslyntours.co.uk).

DECIPHERING THE DA VINCI CODE

The success of Dan Brown's novel *The Da Vinci Code* and the subsequent Hollywood film has seen a flood of visitors descend on Scotland's most beautiful and enigmatic church – **Rosslyn Chapel** (☎ 440 2159; www.rosslynchapel.com; Roslin; adult/child £7.50/free; 9.30am-6pm Mon-Sat, noon-4.45pm Sun Apr-Sep, 9.30am-5pm Mon-Sat, noon-4.45pm Sun Oct-Mar; 15). The chapel was built in the mid-15th century for William St Clair, third earl of Orkney, and the ornately carved interior – at odds with the architectural fashion of its time – is a monument to the mason's art, rich in symbolic imagery. As well as flowers, vines, angels and biblical figures, the carved stones include many examples of the pagan 'Green Man'; other figures are associated with Freemasonry and the Knights Templar. Intriguingly, there are also carvings of plants from the Americas that predate Columbus' voyage of discovery. The symbolism of these images has led some researchers to conclude that Rosslyn is some kind of secret Templar repository, and it has been claimed that hidden vaults beneath the chapel could conceal anything from the Holy Grail or the head of John the Baptist to the body of Christ himself.

The chapel is on the eastern edge of the village of Roslin, seven miles south of Edinburgh's centre. **Celtic Trails** (☎ 448 2869; www.celtic-trails.co.uk) offers half-/full-day tours of the chapel and surrounding area for £33/60 per person, not including admission fees.

☉ UNION CANAL

Fountainbridge; 1, 34 or 35

Built 200 years ago and abandoned in the 1960s, the Union Canal was restored and reopened to navigation in 2002. **Edinburgh Quays**, its city-centre terminus in Tollcross, is now a focus for redevelopment and a starting point for canal cruises, walks and bike rides. The canal stretches west for 31 miles through the rural landscape of West Lothian to Falkirk, where it joins the Forth and Clyde Canal at the Falkirk Wheel boat lift.

At Harrison Park, a mile to the west of Edinburgh Quays, is a pretty little basin with **rowing boats** (per hr £3.50; 11am-5pm Sun Apr-Sep) belonging to the Edinburgh Canal Society. Here, too, you'll find the canal-boat restaurant Zazou (p120).

 **Amy Hickman**
Works for bikeclub.org.uk, an organisation that encourages young people to take up cycling

Is cycling a good way to explore Edinburgh? Definitely, the network of cycle routes is great, mostly on old railway lines so the hills are pretty easy. You can hire a bike and cycle map from somewhere like Biketrax (p114) and see loads of the city in a day. **Some good routes?** The Union Canal towpath (p112) is good, and the Water of Leith Walkway (p99) is perfect for exploring – it leads from the Scottish National Gallery of Modern Art (p98) through Stockbridge to the Shore (p129), not far from the Royal Yacht Britannia (p128). **Where would you recommend for a drink or a bite to eat?** The Engine Shed (p117), near the Innocent Railway cycle path (my favourite ride), is a good refuelling stop. Down in Leith, I often go for a drink at the Roseleaf (p134) or Café Truva (p131). And if the weather's good, it's nice to sit outside at Teuchters Landing (p131).

Commuters travel through the peaceful Meadows (p109)

SHOP

BACKBEAT Music
☎ 668 2666; 31 E Crosscauseway;
🕑 10am-5.30pm Mon-Sat; 🚌 42
If you're hunting for secondhand vinyl from way back, this cramped little shop has a stunning and constantly changing collection of jazz, blues, rock and soul, plus lots of '60s and '70s stuff, though you have to take some time to hunt through the clutter.

BIKETRAX Bicycles
☎ 228 6633; www.biketrax.co.uk; 11-13 Lochin Pl; 🕑 9.30am-6pm Mon-Fri, 9.30am-5.30pm Sat, noon-5pm Sun; 🚌 all Tollcross buses
This backstreet bike shop and workshop combined is the place in Edinburgh to come and lust after the latest models from Trek, Genesis and Ridgeback, or to kit yourself out in the latest lycra. They also hire bikes (from £12 a day) and sell cycle maps of Edinburgh so you can explore the city on two wheels.

BOARDWISE Outdoor Sports
☎ 229 5887; www.boardwise.com; 4 Lady Lawson St; 🕑 10am-6pm Mon-Sat; 🚌 2 or 35

Boardwise supplies all the gear – and the cool threads – you'll need for any board-based sports, be it snow, skate or surf.

🗋 COURTYARD ANTIQUES *Antiques*

☎ 662 9008; 108a Causewayside; ⏱ 9.30am-5.30pm daily; 🚌 42

Hidden down a lane, the Courtyard has two crowded floors of wooden furniture (19th century to the 1970s), toys and militaria, including some fascinating bric-a-brac that ranges from 78rpm records to a homemade canvas canoe.

🗋 GREENSLEEVES *Fashion*

☎ 447 8042; 203 Morningside Rd; ⏱ 10am-5.30pm Mon-Sat; 🚌 5, 11, 15, 16, 17 or 23

If you want to buy a designer dress without breaking the bank, have a flick through the racks at Greensleeves, which specialises in high-quality secondhand clothes, handbags and shoes, many with designer labels.

🗋 HOGS HEAD *Music*

☎ 667 5274; www.hogs-head.com; 62 South Clerk St; ⏱ 10am-5.30pm Mon-Sat, 1-5pm Sun; 🚌 all Newington buses

A classic, old-skool music and film shop that buys and sells secondhand CDs and DVDs. Thousands of disks and box sets to browse among, a good range of T-shirts, and staff who know whereof they speak.

🗋 KILBERRY BAGPIPES *Scottish*

☎ 668 3303; www.kilberry.com; 93 Causewayside; ⏱ 9am-5pm Mon-Fri, 9am-1pm Sat; 🚌 42

Makers and retailers of traditional Highland bagpipes, Kilberry also sells piping accessories, snare drums, books, CDs and learning materials.

Kilberry Bagpipes, for all your Highland gear

NEIGHBOURHOODS

SOUTH EDINBURGH

☐ MEADOWS POTTERY *Crafts*
☎ 662 4064; www.themeadowspottery
.com; 11a Summerhall Pl; ⏱ 10.30am-
5pm Mon-Sat; 🚍 42

This little shop sells a range of
colourful, high-fired oxidised
stoneware, both domestic and
decorative, all hand-thrown on the
premises. If you can't find what
you want, you can commission
custom-made pieces.

☐ PECKHAM'S *Food & Drink*
☎ 229 7054; www.peckhams.co.uk;
155-159 Bruntsfield Pl; ⏱ 8am-
midnight daily; 🚍 all Bruntsfield buses

Peckham's is a busy neighbourhood deli selling all the usual deli
stuff: smoked salmon, gravadlax

and kippers, all kinds of cheeses,
freshly made bread and sandwiches, and organic veggies. There's
also a great selection of wines and
whiskies, and you can buy booze
here until 10pm, seven days a week.

☐ WEST PORT BOOKS
Secondhand Books
☎ 229 4431; 147 West Port;
⏱ 10.30am-5.30pm Mon, Thu & Fri,
noon-5.30pm Tue, Wed & Sat; 🚍 2 or 35

A long-established secondhand
bookshop, West Port has a good
range of material covering Scottish history and also specialises in
titles covering Indian and Hima-
layan history and art. There's a 10%
discount for students.

Spoiled for choice at Peckham's

WORD POWER *Books*

☎ 662 9112; www.word-power.co.uk; 43 W Nicolson St; ⏰ 10am-6pm Mon-Fri, 10.30am-6pm Sat, noon-5pm Sun; 🚌 all South Bridge buses

A radical independent bookshop that supports small publishers and local writers, Word Power stocks a wide range of political, gay and feminist literature, as well as non-mainstream fiction and nonfiction.

EAT

ANN PURNA
Vegetarian   £-££

☎ 662 1807; 45 St Patrick's Sq; ⏰ noon-2pm & 5.30-11pm Mon-Fri, 5.30-11pm Sat & Sun; 🚌 42; **Ⓥ**

This little gem serves vegetarian dishes from southern India in a bright, unfussy dining room enlivened by a few homely decorations. If you're new to this kind of food, opt for a *thali* – a self-contained platter that contains two starters, four different curry dishes, rice, *puri* (puffed bread) and a dessert.

BUFFALO GRILL
American   ££-£££

☎ 667 7427; www.buffalogrill.co.uk; 12-14 Chapel St; ⏰ 6-10.30pm Mon-Fri, 5.30-10.30pm Sat, 5-10.15pm Sun; 🚌 42

The Buffalo Grill is cramped, noisy, fun and always busy, with an American-style menu offering burgers, steaks and side orders of fries and onion rings, along with fish and chicken dishes, prawn tempura and vegetarian burgers, but steaks are the main event. BYOB – corkage £1 per bottle of wine or 50p per beer.

ENGINE SHED
Vegetarian   £

☎ 662 0040; www.theengineshed.org; 19 St Leonard's Lane; ⏰ 10am-4pm Mon-Sat; 🚌 2; ♿

This Fairtrade, organic vegetarian cafe is an ideal spot for a healthy lunch, or a cuppa and a bakery-fresh scone after climbing Arthur's Seat. It's been set up to help special-needs adults and as well as having their own bakery they also make their own tofu, which is used plentifully in their tasty curries.

FIRST COAST
Scottish/International   ££

☎ 313 4404; www.first-coast.co.uk; 99-101 Dalry Rd; ⏰ noon-2pm & 5-10.30pm Mon-Sat; 🚌 2, 3, 4, 25, 33 or 44

Our favourite neighbourhood bistro, First Coast has a striking main dining area with pale-grey wood panelling and stripped stone, and a short and simple menu offering hearty comfort food such as slow braised ox cheek with sherry gravy and creamy mash, and wild mushroom gnocchi. At lunch, and from 5pm to 6.30pm, you can have an excellent two-course meal for £11.

JASPER'S Cafe £

☎ 229 8944; www.jaspersjuice.com; 1 Grove St; ⏰ 7am-4pm Mon-Fri, 9am-2pm Sat; 🚌 2; V

This bright cafe specialises in juices and smoothies, from citrus blast (orange, grapefruit and lemon) to beetroot zinger (beetroot, apple and lemon), and serves superb Fairtrade coffee. Breakfast is available till noon, and includes porridge with a choice of toppings (honey, jam or banana), omelettes, cereals and fry-ups, plus lunches of soup, sandwiches, scones and pastries.

KALPNA Indian £-££

☎ 667 9890; www.kalpnarestaurant .com; 2-3 St Patrick Sq; ⏰ noon-2pm & 5.30-11pm Mon-Sat year-round, 6-10.30pm Sun May-Sep; 🚌 all South Bridge buses; V

One of the best Indian restaurants in the country, vegetarian or otherwise, Kalpna serves mostly Gujarati cuisine with a smattering of dishes from other parts of India – try the *khumb masala* (spiced mushrooms in a coconut milk, tomato, garlic and coriander sauce). Specials include the buffet lunch (£7) and a vegan thali (£13.50).

KATIE'S DINER
American ££

☎ 229 1394; www.katiesdiner.com; 12 Barclay Tce; ⏰ 6-9pm Tue-Thu, 6-9.30pm Fri & Sat; 🚌 all Bruntsfield buses

As you might expect from a place run by a husband-and-wife team, this cute little diner has a warm, welcome and homely atmosphere. The handful of tables enjoy a view onto the parkland of Bruntsfield Links, and the menu runs from barbecue chicken wings and nachos to prime Scottish steaks and juicy homemade burgers with fries and coleslaw.

KEBAB MAHAL Asian £

☎ 667 5214; www.kebab-mahal.co.uk; 7 Nicolson Sq; ⏰ noon-midnight Sun-Thu, to 2am Fri & Sat; 🚌 all South Bridge buses

Sophisticated it ain't, but this is the Holy Grail of kebab shops – quality shish kebab and tandoori dishes washed down with chilled lassi for around seven quid. It's a basic cafeteria-style place with a stainless-steel counter and glaring fluorescent lights, but the menu is 100% halal (the Edinburgh Mosque is just 100m along the road) and the kebabs and curries are authentic and delicious.

LEVEN'S Thai Fusion ££

☎ 229 8988; 30-32 Leven St; ⏰ noon-2.30pm & 5-10.30pm Sun-Thu, noon-10.30pm Fri & Sat; 🚌 all Bruntsfield buses

From the spectacular chandeliers and slowly pulsing blue/purple mood lighting to the designer colour palette and Villeroy and Boch tableware, everything about this restaurant oozes style. The food lives up to the surroundings, with clever and unexpected combinations of flavours, colours and textures in dishes such as lamb spring roll with a Thai curry sauce.

🍴 MCKIRDY'S STEAKHOUSE
Scottish ££-£££

☎ 229 6660; www.mckirdyssteakhouse .co.uk; 151 Morrison St; ☷ 5.30-10pm Sun-Thu, 5-10.30pm Fri & Sat; 🚍 2; 🚹

The McKirdy brothers – owners of a local butcher's business established in 1895 – have cut out the middleman and now run one of Edinburgh's best steakhouses. The friendly staff here serve up starters – such as haggis with Drambuie sauce – and juicy, perfectly cooked steaks from rump to T-bone, accompanied by mustard mash or crispy fries. There's a kids' menu, and you can get a two-course early dinner (until 6.30pm) for £13.

🍴 MOSQUE KITCHEN
Indian £

☎ 667 1777; 50 Potter Row; ☷ noon-7pm Sat-Thu, noon-1pm & 1.45-7pm Fri; 🚍 42

Sophisticated it ain't – expect shared tables and disposable plates – but this is the place to go for cheap, authentic and delicious homemade curries, kebabs, pakora and naan bread washed down with lassi or mango juice. Caters to Edinburgh's Central Mosque, but welcomes all – local students have taken to it big time. No alcohol.

🍴 POINT RESTAURANT
Scottish ££

☎ 221 5555; Point Hotel, 34 Bread St; ☷ noon-2pm & 6-10pm Mon-Fri, 6-10pm Sat, 6-9pm Sun; 🚍 2 or 35

The Point Restaurant's lunch and dinner menus offer exceptional value – delicious Scottish/international cuisine served by attentive, smartly clad staff in an elegant room with dark-wood furniture, proper linen napkins and art deco chandeliers. With a three-course dinner at £22 and house wine at £15 a bottle, reservations are strongly recommended.

🍴 ROTI *Indian*
££-£££

☎ 221 9998; 73 Morrison St; ☷ noon-2.30pm Mon-Sat, 5pm-midnight daily; 🚍 13, 19, 37 or 41

This is no ordinary Indian restaurant, but an intimate, minimalist space with low lighting, colourful drapes and the hot pink of fresh fuchsia flowers. The menu is intriguing, offering dishes that lie well off the beaten curry trail, such as lamb and mint broth with herb dumplings and Goan fish curry (sour, salt and sweet all at the same time).

☗ SURUCHI *Indian* ££

☎ 556 6583; 14a Nicolson St; ☽ noon-2.30pm & 5-11pm; 🚍 all South Bridge buses

A laidback Indian eatery with handmade turquoise tiles, lazy ceiling fans and chilled-out jazz guitar, Suruchi offers a range of exotic dishes as well as the traditional tandoori standards, many with a Scottish twist. An amusing touch is added by menu descriptions translated into broad Scots ('a beezer o' a curry this…gey nippie oan the tongue').

☗ SUSHIYA *Japanese* ££

☎ 313 3222; 19 Dalry Rd; ☽ noon-2.30pm & 5-10.30pm Sun, Mon, Wed & Thu, noon-11pm Fri & Sat; 🚍 2, 3, 4, 25, 33 or 44

The neat, geometric decor in this pleasingly smart little sushi bar – square hardwood tables with black-leather stools and square light fittings, set against white walls, wasabi-green doors and brushed steel – is mirrored in the neat, geometric portions of market-fresh tuna, salmon, scallop and octopus prepared to order by the smiling Mr Yuen. Other options include teriyaki beef and chicken, udon noodles and ramen soup.

☗ SWEET MELINDAS *Scottish* £££

☎ 229 7953; www.sweetmelindas .co.uk; 11 Roseneath St; ☽ noon-2pm & 6-10pm Tue-Sat, 6-10pm Mon; 🚍 24 or 41; Ⓥ

With ingredients sourced from the fishmonger next door and the vegetable market around the corner, and everything from the bread to the chocolate truffles handmade in the kitchen, Sweet Melindas offers a true taste of Scottish home cooking. The ambience is chilled and the menu concentrates on seafood, with at least one vegetarian starter and main.

☗ THAI LEMONGRASS *Thai* ££

☎ 229 2225; 40-41 Bruntsfield Pl; ☽ noon-2.30pm & 5-11.30pm Mon-Thu, noon-11.30pm Fri & Sat, 1-11.30pm Sun; 🚍 all Bruntsfield buses

From the waiter's prayerlike gesture of greeting to the gold Buddha gazing down on the diners, everything about this restaurant feels authentically Thai. The rustic decor of terracotta tiles, yellow walls and cane tablemats makes for a relaxing atmosphere, while the rich and varied flavours of the food – fiery chilli, fragrant lemongrass, tangy lime leaves and sweet coconut – will keep you coming back for more.

☗ ZAZOU *Scottish/French* £££

☎ 669 3294; www.zazoucruises.co.uk; Union Canal, Ogilvie Tce, Polwarth; ☽ booking only; 🚍 38

How's this for dinner with a difference – hire a whole canal boat and cruise along the Union Canal as you dine. The menu varies, but offers a choice of four to six starters and main courses, including one fish and one vegetarian option. Book at least seven days in advance; groups of six or more (maximum 12) can have the boat to themselves.

DRINK

☛ ATHLETIC ARMS (THE DIGGERS) Pub

☎ 337 3822; www.theathleticarms.co.uk; 1-3 Angle Park Tce; ☺ noon-midnight Mon-Thu, noon-1am Fri & Sat, 12.30-6pm Sun; ☒ 1, 28 or 34
Named for the cemetery across the street (the grave-diggers used to nip in and slake their thirst after a hard day's interring), the Diggers dates from 1897. Its heyday as a real-ale drinker's mecca has passed, but the beer is still good, the decor has barely changed in 100 years, and it's packed to the gills with football and rugby fans on match days.

☛ AULD HOOSE Pub

☎ 668 2934; www.theauldhoose.co.uk; 23-25 St Leonards St; ☺ noon-12.45am Mon-Sat, 12.30pm-12.45am Sun; ☒ 2
Promoting itself as the Southside's only 'alternative' pub, the Auld Hoose certainly lives up to its reputation with unpretentious, old-fashioned decor, a range of real ales from remote Scottish microbreweries (Trashy Blonde from Brewdog on Arran, Avalanche Ale from Loch Fyne in Argyll), and a juke box that would make the late John Peel weep with joy.

☛ BENNET'S BAR Pub

☎ 229 5143; 8 Leven St; ☺ 11am-12.30am Mon-Wed, 11am-1am Thu-Sat, 12.30-11.30pm Sun; ☒ all Tollcross buses
Bennet's has managed to retain almost all of its beautiful Victorian fittings, from the leaded stained-glass windows and ornate mirrors to the wooden gantry and brass water taps on the bar. If whisky is your poison, there are over 100 malts to choose from.

☛ BLUE BLAZER Pub

☎ 229 5030; 2 Spittal St; ☺ 11am-1am Mon-Sat, 12.30pm-1am Sun; ☒ 2 or 35
With its bare wooden floors, cosy fireplace and efficient bar staff, the Blue Blazer is a down-to-earth antidote to the designer excess of modern style bars, catering to a loyal clientele of real-ale enthusiasts, pie eaters and Saturday horse-racing fans.

☛ BRAUHAUS Bar

☎ 656 0356; 105 Lauriston Pl; ☺ noon-1am; ☒ 23, 27, 35, 45
The bar itself is fairly small – half a dozen bar stools, a couple of sofas

NEIGHBOURHOODS

SOUTH EDINBURGH

Which whisky to choose? Pondering the decision at Bennet's Bar (p121)

and a scattering of seats – but the ambition is sizeable, with a vast menu of bottled beers from all over the world, ranging from the usual suspects from Belgium, Germany and the Czech Republic, to more unusual brews such as Paradox Smokehead (a 10% ABV stout aged for six months in a whisky cask).

CALEY SAMPLE ROOM *Pub*
☎ 337 7204; www.thecaleysampleroom
.co.uk; 58 Angle Park Tce; ☒ 11am-
midnight Mon-Thu, 11am-1am Fri & Sat,
12.30pm-midnight Sun; ☒ 4, 28, 34,
35 or 44

The Sample Room is a big, lively, convivial pub serving a wide range of wines and excellent real ales,

and some of the best pub grub in the city. It's popular with sports fans too, who gather to watch football and rugby matches on the large-screen TVs.

CANNY MAN'S *Pub*
☎ 447 1484; 237 Morningside Rd;
☒ 11.30am-11pm Mon-Wed, 11.30am-
midnight Thu-Sat, 12.30pm-11pm Sun;
☒ 11, 15, 16, 17 or 23

A lovably eccentric pub, the Canny Man's is made up of a crowded warren of tiny rooms that are crammed with a bizarre collection of antiques and curiosities (a description that could also apply to some of the regulars), and where the landlord regularly refuses entry to anyone who looks scruffy, inebriated or vaguely pinko/commie/subversive. If you can get in here, you'll find it serves excellent real ale, vintage port and Cuban cigars.

CLOISTERS *Pub*

☎ 221 9997; 26 Brougham St; ☼ noon-midnight Sun-Thu, to 12.30am Fri & Sat; 🚌 24

Housed in a converted manse (minister's house) that once belonged to the next-door church, and furnished with well-worn, mismatched wooden tables and chairs, Cloisters now ministers to a mixed congregation of students, locals and real-ale connoisseurs. It has decent grub and coffee, and a nice warm fireplace in winter.

DRAGONFLY *Cocktail Bar*

☎ 228 4543; www.dragonflycocktail bar.com; 52 West Port; ☼ noon-1am; 🚌 2; 📶

A super-stylish lounge bar with a Raffles of Singapore vibe – it's all crystal chandeliers, polished wood and oriental art – Dragonfly has won rave reviews both for its innovative cocktails and its designer decor. Grab a seat in the neat little mezzanine, from where you can look down on the bar as the Singapore Slings are being slung.

PEAR TREE HOUSE *Pub*

☎ 667 7533; 38 W Nicolson St; ☼ 11am-midnight Mon-Thu, 11am-1am Fri & Sat, 12.30pm-midnight Sun; 🚌 2, 41 or 42

The Pear Tree is another student favourite, with comfy sofas and board games inside, plus the city centre's biggest beer garden outside. There's a Monday-night quiz and live music in the garden on Sunday afternoons in the summer.

SOUTHSIDER *Pub*

☎ 667 2003; 3-7 W Richmond St; ☼ noon-midnight Mon-Thu, noon-1am Fri & Sat, 12.30pm-midnight Sun; 🚌 all Newington buses; 📶

Always busy with students and regulars, the Southsider is a big, old-fashioned, slightly rough-around-the-edges pub that pulls in people from further afield with a good selection of real ales, table football, Wednesday-night pub quizzes, and live music on Thursday, Saturday and Sunday.

PLAY

CAMEO *Cinema*

☎ 228 2800; www.picturehouses.co.uk; 38 Home St; adult/child £6.80/4.50; 🚌 10, 11, 15, 16 or 17

The independently owned Cameo is a good old-fashioned cinema showing an imaginative mix of mainstream as well as art-house

movies. There is a good programme of midnight movies, Sunday matinees and special events.

⭐ **DOMINION** *Cinema*
☎ 447 4771; www.dominioncinemas
.net; 18 Newbattle Tce; adult/child
£7.20/4.90; 🚍 11, 15, 16, 17 or 23
The much-loved Dom is a delightful, independent, family-run
four-screener in a 1938 art deco
building. The programme is
unashamedly mainstream and
family-oriented, and popular films
often have a good old-fashioned
intermission so you can buy an ice
cream halfway through.

⭐ **EDINBURGH FESTIVAL
THEATRE** *Theatre*
☎ 529 6000; www.eft.co.uk; 13-29
Nicolson St; tickets £8-50; 🕐 box office
10am-6pm Mon-Sat, to 8pm on show
nights; 🚍 all South Bridge buses
The modern glass-and-steel facade of the Festival Theatre hides
a lovely art deco auditorium,
the city's main venue for ballet,
contemporary dance and opera.
It also stages musicals, concerts,
drama and children's shows, and
performances by the critically
acclaimed Scottish Ballet.

⭐ **KING'S THEATRE** *Theatre*
☎ 529 6000; www.eft.co.uk; 2 Leven St;
tickets £10-30; 🕐 box office open 1hr
before show; 🚍 all Tollcross buses

The King's is a traditional family theatre with a programme of
musicals, drama, comedy and
its famous annual Christmas
pantomime.

⭐ **QUEEN'S HALL** *Music*
☎ 668 2019; www.thequeenshall.net;
Clerk St; tickets £10-30; 🕐 box office
10am-5.30pm Mon-Sat, or to 15min
after show begins; 🚍 all Newington
buses
The Queen's Hall is home to the
Scottish Chamber Orchestra, but
it also hosts jazz concerts, tribute
bands and a whole range of other
events.

⭐ **ROYAL COMMONWEALTH
POOL** *Health & Fitness*
☎ 667 7211; www.edinburghleisure.co
.uk; 21 Dalkeith Rd; adult/child
£4.20/1.80; 🕐 6am-9.30pm Mon-Fri,
10am-4.30pm Sat & Sun, closed 9-10am
Wed; 🚍 2, 14, 30 or 33
This is the city's main swimming
facility, which was built for the
1970 Commonwealth Games. It
has a 50m Olympic pool, diving
pool, children's pool, flumes
and fitness centre. Closed for
refurbishment at time of research,
it is scheduled to reopen summer
2011.

⭐ **STEREO** *Club*
☎ 229 9438; www.stereonightclub
.co.uk; 28 King's Stables Rd; 🚍 28

Stereo pulls in a pissed-up, dance-till-you-puke crowd, who queue up for the weekly **Shagtag** (admission £5; 🕒 10pm-3am Tue), a hugely successful student night which involves a complicated snogging-by-numbers event. Weekends are devoted to party nights, with the crowds gamely thrashing away to a soundtrack of pop, funk, disco and house while trying not to barf up the gallon of cheap promo drinks they just downed.

⭐ **WEE RED BAR** *Club*
☎ 229 1442; www.weeredbar.co.uk; **Edinburgh College of Art, 74 Lauriston Pl;** 🚌 23, 27, 35 or 45
The Wee Red Bar has been around so long there's a danger the authorities will slap a blue plaque on it and declare it a national monument. Wee, red and frequented, hardly surprisingly, by lots of art students, it's famous for the **Egg** (admission £5; 🕒 11pm-3am Sat), a weekly smorgasbord of classic punk, ska, northern soul, indie etc that is still one of the best club nights in the city.

>LEITH & THE WATERFRONT

Two miles northeast of the city centre, Leith has been Edinburgh's seaport since the 14th century, and remained an independent burgh with its own town council until it was incorporated by the city during the 1920s. Like many of Britain's dockland areas, it fell into decay in the decades following WWII but has been undergoing a steady revival since the late 1980s. Old warehouses have been turned into luxury flats, and a lush crop of trendy bars and restaurants has sprouted up along the waterfront.

The city council has formulated a major redevelopment plan for the entire Edinburgh waterfront from Leith to Granton, the first phase of which is the Ocean Terminal, a shopping and leisure complex that includes the former Royal Yacht Britannia and a berth for visiting cruise liners. Parts of Leith are still a bit rough, but it's a distinctive corner of the city and well worth exploring.

LEITH & THE WATERFRONT

◉ SEE
Leith Links 1   F4
Newhaven Harbour 2   B1
Royal Yacht Britannia 3   D1
Sea-fari 4   B1
Shore 5   E2
Trinity House 6   E3

⬠ SHOP
Edinburgh Architectural
    Salvage Yard 7   C3
Flux 8   E3

Georgian Antiques 9   F3
Kinloch Anderson 10   D2
Ocean Terminal 11   D2
Tiso Outdoor
    Experience 12   D2

🍴 EAT
A Room In Leith 13   E2
Café Truva 14   E3
Daniel's Bistro 15   D2
Diner 7 16   E2
Fishers Bistro 17   E2
Khublai Khan 18   E3

Kitchin 19   E2
Loch Fyne 20   B1
Restaurant Martin
    Wishart 21   E3
Shore 22   E2
Vintners Rooms 23   E3

🍸 DRINK
Carriers Quarters 24   E2
Old Chain Pier 25   A2
Port O'Leith 26   E3
Roseleaf 27   D3
Starbank Inn 28   A2

SEE

⊙ CRAMOND VILLAGE

Cramond Glebe Rd; 🚌 24 or 41

With its moored yachts, stately swans and whitewashed houses clustered around the mouth of the River Almond, Cramond is the most picturesque corner of Edinburgh. It's also rich in history – the Romans built a fort here in the 2nd century AD. Originally a mill village, Cramond has a 17th-century church, a 15th-century tower house and a local history museum in **The Maltings** (☎ 312 6034; Cramond Village; admission free; ⊙ 2-5pm Sat & Sun Jun-Sep, daily during Edinburgh Festival), but most visitors come to enjoy a walk along the river or to enjoy a meal or a drink at the **Cramond Inn** (☎ 336 2035; 30 Cramond Glebe Rd).

⊙ LEITH LINKS

🚌 21, 25, 34 or 49

This public park was originally common grazing land, but is more famous as the birthplace of modern golf. Although St Andrews has the oldest golf course in the world, it was at Leith Links in 1744 that the first official rules of the game were formulated by the Honorable Company of Edinburgh Golfers. A stone cairn on the western side of the park bears a plaque describing how the ancient game was played over five holes of around 400 yards each.

OVER THE SEA TO INCHCOLM

The tiny island of Inchcolm is home to the ruins of **Inchcolm Abbey** (☎ 0138-3823-332; Inchcolm, Fife; adult/child £4.50/2.25; ⊙ 9.30am-5.30pm Apr-Sep), one of Scotland's best-preserved medieval abbeys, as well as colonies of grey seals, puffins and other seabirds. You can visit Inchcolm from Newhaven Harbour (below) or Queensferry (p129).

⊙ NEWHAVEN HARBOUR

Newhaven Pl; 🚌 7, 10, 11 or 16

Newhaven was once a distinctive fishing community whose fishwives tramped the streets of Edinburgh's New Town selling *caller herrin* (fresh herring) from wicker creels on their backs. Modern development has dispelled the fishing-village atmosphere, but the little harbour still boasts its picturesque lighthouse. **Sea.fari** (☎ 331 4857; www.seafari.co.uk) runs high-speed boat trips (adult/child £22/19) from the harbour to Inchcolm Island (above).

⊙ ROYAL YACHT BRITANNIA

☎ 555 5566; www.royalyachtbritannia.co.uk; Ocean Terminal; adult/child £11/7; ⊙ 9.30am-4.30pm Jul-Sep, 10am-4pm Apr-Jun & Oct, 10am-3.30pm Nov-Mar, last admission 1½hr before closing; 🚌 1, 11, 22, 34, 35 or 36; ♿

The Royal Yacht Britannia was the royal family's home-away-from-home during their foreign travels from her launch in 1953 until her decommissioning in 1997. Now permanently moored at Ocean Terminal, she is a floating monument to the Queen's tastes and predilections. For more details see p22.

For more details see p22.

◉ THE SHORE
🚌 16, 22, 35 or 36

The most attractive part of Leith is the cobbled waterfront street alongside the Water of Leith, lined with pubs and restaurants. Before the docks were built in the 19th century this was Leith's original wharf. An iron plaque in front of No 30 marks the King's Landing – the spot where King George IV (the first reigning British monarch to visit Scotland since Charles II in 1650) stepped ashore in 1822.

◉ TRINITY HOUSE
☎ 554 3289; www.trinityhouseleith.org.uk; 99 Kirkgate; admission free; 🕑 guided tours 1-3pm Sat; all Leith Walk buses

This neoclassical building dating from 1816 was the headquarters

CRUISING AROUND QUEENSFERRY

Queensferry is a lively and attractive seaside village with cobbled lanes, 18th-century terraced houses and a picturesque little harbour, situated 8 miles west of the city centre. It served as a port for ferries to Fife until 1964 when the graceful Forth Rd Bridge – now the fifth longest in Europe – was opened. The even more spectacular Forth Bridge, which carries the railway on three huge cantilevers, dates from 1890. **Queensferry Museum** (☎ 331 5545; 53 High St; admission free; 🕑 10am-1pm & 2.15-5pm Mon & Thu-Sat, noon-5pm Sun; 🚌 First Edinburgh 43) contains interesting information on the building of the Forth bridges, and fascinating photographs of the railway bridge in various stages of construction.

The ferry **Maid of the Forth** (☎ 331 4857; www.maidoftheforth.co.uk; return adult/child £14.70/5.85, incl admission to Inchcolm Abbey) sails from Queensferry to Inchcolm (opposite), one to four times daily most days from May to October. Two miles west of Queensferry lies **Hopetoun House** (☎ 331 2451; www.hopetounhouse.com; adult/child £8/4.25; 🕑 10.30am-5pm Easter-Sep, last admission 4pm), one of Scotland's finest stately homes.

There are several good pubs and restaurants in Queensferry, including the 350-year-old **Hawes Inn** (☎ 331 1990; Newhalls Rd; 🕑 11am-11pm Mon-Sat, 12.30-10.30pm Sun; 🚌 First Edinburgh 43) opposite the Inchcolm ferry, which is famously mentioned in Robert Louis Stevenson's novel Kidnapped, and **Orocco Pier** (☎ 331 1298; 17 High St; 🕑 11am-midnight Sun-Thu, 11am-1am Fri & Sat; 🚌 First Edinburgh 43), a stylish and modern bar-restaurant with an outdoor terrace that has stunning views of the road and rail bridges. Food is served from 9am to 10pm.

The cobbled waterfront of The Shore (p129)

of the Incorporation of Masters and Mariners (founded in 1380), the nautical equivalent of a tradesmen's guild, and is a treasure house of old ship models, navigation instruments and nautical memorabilia relating to Leith's maritime history. Tours also available Tuesday to Friday by booking ahead.

SHOP

EDINBURGH ARCHITECTURAL SALVAGE YARD *Antiques*

☎ 554 7077; www.easy-arch-salv.co.uk; 31 West Bowling Green St; 🕙 9am-5pm Mon-Fri, noon-5pm Sat; 🚍 1, 10, 32 or 34

A happy hunting ground for house renovators, this is a rich source of period features where you can find everything from original Georgian and Victorian cast-iron fireplaces and kitchen ranges to roll-top baths and gleaming, chrome, art deco bathroom fittings.

FLUX *Arts & Crafts*

☎ 554 4075; www.get2flux.co.uk; 55 Bernard St; 🕙 11am-6pm Mon-Sat & noon-5pm Sun; 🚍 16, 22, 35 or 36

Flux is an outlet for contemporary British and overseas arts and crafts, including stained glass, metalware, jewellery and ceramics, all ethically sourced and many made using recycled materials.

🏛 GEORGIAN ANTIQUES
Antiques

☎ 553 7286; www.georgianantiques
.net; 10 Pattison St; ⏰ 8.30am-5.30pm
Mon-Fri, 10am-2pm Sat; 🚌 12, 16 or 35
This place has the largest selection of antiques in Scotland,
with three floors of Victorian and
Edwardian furniture, clocks, brass,
porcelain, mirrors, light fittings
and paintings.

🏛 KINLOCH ANDERSON
Scottish

☎ 555 1390; www.kinlochanderson
.com; 4 Dock St; ⏰ 9am-5pm Mon-Sat;
🚌 16, 22, 35 or 36
Founded in 1868 and still family-
run, Kinloch Anderson is the main
supplier of kilts and Highland
dress to the royal family. They can
find out your clan tartan and kit
you out in formal or semiformal
Highland dress, or even tartan
trousers.

🏛 OCEAN TERMINAL *Mall*

☎ 555 8888; www.oceanterminal.com;
Ocean Dr; ⏰ 10am-8pm Mon-Fri, 10am-
7pm Sat, 11am-6pm Sun; 🚌 1, 11, 22,
34, 35 or 36
Anchored by Debenhams and BHS
department stores, Ocean Terminal is the biggest shopping centre
in Edinburgh; fashion outlets
include Fat Face, GAP, Schuh, Top
Shop and White Stuff.

🏛 TISO OUTDOOR
EXPERIENCE *Outdoor Sports*

☎ 554 0804; www.tiso.com; 41 Commercial St; ⏰ 9am-6pm Mon, Tue, Fri &
Sat, 9.30am-6pm Wed, 9am-7.30pm Thu,
11am-5pm Sun; 🚌 16, 22, 35 or 36
The macho cousin of Tiso's city
centre store, here you can try before
you buy with their Goretex-testing
shower, boot-bashing footpath,
rock-climbing wall, ice-climbing
wall and stove-testing area.

🍴 EAT

🍴 A ROOM IN LEITH
Scottish   ££

☎ 554 7427; www.aroomin.co.uk; 1c
Dock Pl; ⏰ noon-2pm & 5.30-10pm;
🚌 16, 22, 35 or 36
This restaurant (and its companion
bar, Teuchters Landing) inhabits a
warren of nooks and crannies in a
red-brick building (once a waiting
room for ferries across the Firth of
Forth), with a bright conservatory
and outdoor tables on a floating
terrace in the dock. The Scottish-
flavoured menu includes haggis
with mustard-and-thyme cream
sauce, and roast venison with red
onion tart and port gravy.

🍴 CAFÉ TRUVA *Cafe*   £

☎ 554 5502; 77 The Shore; ⏰ 9am-
6.30pm; 🚌 16, 22, 35 or 36
A firm favourite with local Leithers,
Truva combines a standard cafe

menu of breakfast fry-ups, coffee, soups and sandwiches with a tempting array of Turkish specialities, from roast aubergines and tomatoes to hummus and pitta or sweet, sticky baklava.

DANIEL'S BISTRO French ££
☎ 553 5933; www.daniels-bistro.co.uk; 88 Commercial St; ⏰ 10am-10pm; 🚌 16, 22, 35 or 36

Daniel comes from Alsace, and his all-French kitchen staff combine top Scottish and French produce with Gallic know-how to create a wide range of delicious dishes. The Provencal fish soup is excellent, and main courses range from *boeuf bourguignon* (beef and red wine casserole) to *cassoulet* (stew of pork, duck and beans). A seriously filling three-course lunch is just £9.70.

DINER 7 Café ££
☎ 553 0624; www.diner7.co.uk; 7 Commercial St; ⏰ 11am-11pm; 🚌 16, 22, 35 or 36

A neat local eatery with rust-coloured leather booths and banquettes, black and copper tables, and local art on the walls, this diner has a menu of succulent Aberdeen Angus steaks and homemade burgers. Also on offer is more unusual fare such as chicken and chorizo kebabs, or smoked haddock with black pudding stovies.

FISHERS BISTRO
Seafood ££-£££
☎ 554 5666; www.fishersbistros.co.uk; 1 The Shore; ⏰ noon-10.30pm; 🚌 16, 22, 35 or 36

This cosy bar-turned-restaurant, tucked beneath a 17th-century signal tower, is one of the city's best seafood restaurants. The menu ranges in price, from cheaper dishes such as mackerel with beetroot, chilli and orange dressing, to more expensive delights such as North Berwick lobster served with garlic and herb butter. There's another branch in the city centre (p85).

KHUBLAI KHAN
Mongolian ££-£££
☎ 555 0005; www.khublaikhan.co.uk; 43 Assembly St; ⏰ 6-10.30pm daily, 12.30-2.30pm Fri & Sun; 🚌 12, 16 or 35; Ⓥ

OK, the authenticity may be questionable but a Mongolian barbecue certainly makes a change from curry or pizza. Choose from a buffet of raw meat, seafood and vegetables, flavoured with oils, spices and sauces of your choice, and have it cooked to order on a Mongolian-style barbecue (veggies have their own grills).

KITCHIN Scottish £££
☎ 555 1755; www.thekitchin.com; 78 Commercial Quay; ⏰ 12.15-2pm Tue-Sat, 6.30-10pm Tue-Thu, 6.30- 10.30pm Fri & Sat; 🚌 16, 22, 35 or 36

Head to the backstreets to find the delightful Vintners Rooms (p134)

Fresh, seasonal, locally sourced Scottish produce is the philosophy that has won a Michelin star for this elegant but unpretentious restaurant. The menu moves with the seasons, of course, so expect fresh salads in summer and game in winter, and shellfish dishes such as seared scallops with endive *tarte tatin* when there's an 'r' in the month.

🍴 LOCH FYNE *Seafood* ££–£££

☎ 559 3900; www.lochfyne.com; 25 Pier Pl; 🕐 10am-10pm Sun-Thu, 10am-10.30pm Fri & Sat; 🚌 7, 10 or 11

Housed in the old Victorian fish market building next to Newhaven harbour, this stylish restaurant and seafood deli serves up spectacular shellfish platters (£40, enough for two people) of fresh oysters, mussels, scallops, clams, cockles, crab, lobster and langoustines, as well as sustainably fished or farmed salmon, prawns, cod, halibut and haddock.

🍴 RESTAURANT MARTIN WISHART *French/Scottish* £££

☎ 553 3557; www.martin-wishart.co.uk; 54 The Shore; 🕐 noon-2pm & 7-10pm Tue-Sat; 🚌 16, 22, 35 or 36

In 2001 this restaurant became the first in Edinburgh to win a Michelin star. The eponymous chef has worked with Albert Roux, Marco Pierre White and Nick Nairn, and brings a modern French approach to the best Scottish produce, from lobster and smoked haddock soufflé to braised saddle of lamb. A set three-course lunch costs £28.

🍴 SHORE *Seafood* ££–£££

☎ 553 5080; 3-4 The Shore; 🕐 noon-2.30pm & 6-10.30pm daily; 🚌 16, 22, 35 or 36

The atmospheric dining room next door to the popular Shore pub is a haven of wood-panelled peace, with old photographs, nautical knick-knacks, fresh flowers and an open fire adding to the romantic theme. The menu changes daily and specialises in Scottish seafood and game.

VINTNERS ROOMS
French   £££
☎ 554 6767; www.thevintnersrooms .com; The Vaults, 87 Giles St; ⏱ noon- 2pm & 7-10pm Tue-Sat; 🚌 22 or 36

An authentic Georgian wine-merchant's saleroom, beautifully decorated with original 18th-century stucco work (the auctioneer stood in the alcove to the left of the fireplace), forms the beautiful centrepiece of this delightful French restaurant. It's tucked away on a backstreet near the Water of Leith.

DRINK

CARRIERS QUARTERS *Pub*
☎ 554 4122; 42 Bernard St; ⏱ 11am-11pm Sun-Wed, 11am-midnight Thu, 11am-1am Fri & Sat; 🚌 16, 22, 35 or 36

With a low wooden ceiling, stone walls and a fine old fireplace, the Carriers has all the historic atmosphere that its 18th-century origins would imply. It serves real ales and malt whiskies, as well as traditional Scottish bar meals such as stovies and haggis.

OLD CHAIN PIER *Pub*
☎ 552 1233; 32 Trinity Cres; ⏱ noon-11pm Mon-Wed, noon-midnight Thu-Sat, 10am-11pm Sun; 🚌 16 or 32

The delightful Old Chain Pier is an award-winning real ale pub, full of polished wood, brass and nautical paraphernalia and with a brilliant location overlooking the sea. The building was once the 19th-century booking office for steamers across the Firth of Forth (the pier from which it takes its name was washed away in a storm in 1898).

Sunshine and real ale at the Old Chain Pier

▼ PORT O'LEITH *Pub*
☎ 554 3568; 58 Constitution St;
🕒 9am-12.45am Mon-Sat, 12.30pm-
12.45am Sun; 🚌 12, 16 or 35

Open from early in the morning to serve local dock workers, this place is a good, old-fashioned, friendly local boozer with an anchor above the door and a cosy interior swathed with flags and cap bands left behind by visiting sailors (the harbour is just down the road). Pop in for a pint and you'll end up staying here till closing time.

▼ ROSELEAF *Cafe-Bar*
☎ 476 5268; roseleaf.co.uk; 23-24
Sandport Pl; 🕒 10am-1am;
🚌 16, 22, 35 or 36

Cute and quaint and verging on chintzy, the Roseleaf could hardly be further from the average Leith bar. Decked out in flowered wallpaper, old furniture and rose-patterned china, the real ales and bottled beers are complemented by a range of specialty teas, coffees and fruit drinks (including rose lemonade) and well above average pub grub (served 10am to 10pm).

▼ STARBANK INN *Pub*
☎ 552 4141; 64 Laverockbank Rd;
🕒 11am-11pm Mon-Wed, 11am-midnight
Thu-Sat, 12.30-11pm Sun; 🚌 16 or 32

Along with the Old Chain Pier, the Starbank is an oasis of fine ales and good homemade food on Edinburgh's windswept waterfront. There's a conservatory and beer garden at the back and, in winter, a blazing fire to toast your toes in front of.

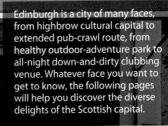

Edinburgh is a city of many faces, from highbrow cultural capital to extended pub-crawl route, from healthy outdoor-adventure park to all-night down-and-dirty clubbing venue. Whatever face you want to get to know, the following pages will help you discover the diverse delights of the Scottish capital.

> Accommodation   138
> Drinking   140
> Food   142
> Architecture   144
> Gay Edinburgh   146
> Kids' Edinburgh   147
> Views   148

NOW OPEN UNTIL 9PM

£1.15

Performers reach out to travellers in Edinburgh's street theatre

ACCOMMODATION

Edinburgh has a wide range of accommodation, from moderately priced guesthouses in lovely Victorian villas and Georgian town houses to luxurious five-star hotels in historic buildings, and an increasing number of stylish boutique hotels. New accommodation is being built at Haymarket, Leith and in the city centre – Apex Hotels recently bought the Georgian building on Waterloo Pl that originally housed Edinburgh's first purpose-built hotel (dating from 1819), and opened it as a luxury boutique hotel in 2009.

Although some older B&Bs and hotels cling to their unreconstructed ways – creaky floorboards, woodchip wallpaper, cardboard toast, and laminated notices ordering you around (NO damp towels on the bed! DO NOT eat food in your room!) – there is a definite trend for even midrange guest houses to raise their game by introducing stylish decor, hotel-style facilities (power showers, wi-fi, flat-screen TVs etc) and gourmet breakfasts.

Places such as Tigerlily, Hotel du Vin and the Hudson Hotel, all recent additions to Edinburgh's growing bevy of boutique hotels, emphasise the trend for converting historic buildings into luxury designer accommodation.

Staying in the Old Town puts you right in the historic heart of Edinburgh, within easy walking distance of the castle, Royal Mile and Holyroodhouse. You'll also be close to lots of good pubs, clubs and restaurants, but there's a dearth of decent midrange options here – most Old Town accommodation is in backpacker hostels or top-end places.

The New Town's accommodation ranges from elegant Georgian guesthouses to the city's newest boutique offerings, all within easy reach of the city's main shopping and restaurant areas.

There's an ever-increasing number of attractive options outside the city centre, with stylish and comfortable guesthouses – many set in Georgian terraces or Victorian villas – in Stockbridge, Morningside, Pilrig and Leith.

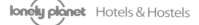 Hotels & Hostels

Need a place to stay? Find and book it at lonelyplanet.com. There are many properties featured for Edinburgh – each personally visited, thoroughly reviewed and happily recommended by a Lonely Planet author. From hostels to high-end hotels, we've hunted out the places that will bring you unique and special experiences. Read independent reviews by authors and other travellers, and get practical information including amenities, maps and photos. Then reserve your room simply and securely via Hotels & Hostels – our online booking service. It's all at lonelyplanet.com/hotels.

Southside and Newington have the city's greatest concentration of good midrange guesthouses and B&Bs, as well as several excellent hotels.

A newish option is the serviced apartment, with places such as **Dreamhouse** (www.dreamhouseapartments.com) and **Knight Residence** (www.theknightresidence .co.uk) offering nightly rates on luxury city-centre flats.

Despite an increase in bed numbers, the city's hotels will still be packed out during the festival period (August and early September) and over Hogmanay (New Year). For these periods, book as far in advance as you can – a year ahead if possible. In general, it's best to book ahead for accommodation at Easter and from mid-May to mid-September. Accommodation might also be in short supply during the Royal Highland Show (late June) and over the weekends when international rugby matches are being played at Murrayfield (two or three weekends from January to March).

Several agencies can help with finding a room, including **VisitScotland** (☎ in the UK 0845 225 5121, outside the UK +44 1506 83212; www.edinburgh.org) and **Festival Beds** (www.festivalbeds.co.uk), which specialises in matching visitors with B&Bs during the August festival period. **Hotel Review Scotland** (www.hotelreviewscotland .com) has lots of independent reviews of Edinburgh hotels.

BEST HOSTELS
> Argyle Backpackers (www.argyle
  -backpackers.co.uk)
> Castle Rock Hostel (www.scotlands-top
  -hostels.com)
> Edinburgh Central Hostel (www
  .edinburghcentral.org)
> Globetrotter Inn (www.globetrotter
  inns.com)
> Smart City Hostel (www.smartcity-
  hostels.com)

COOLEST GUESTHOUSES
> Ardmor House (www.ardmorhouse.com)
> Gerald's Place (www.geraldsplace.com)
> Millers 64 (www.millers64.com)
> Six Mary's Place (www.sixmarysplace
  .co.uk)
> Southside Guest House (www
  .southsideguesthouse.co.uk)

MOST ROMANTIC HOTELS
> Channings (www.channings.co.uk)
> Howard (www.thehoward.com)
> Prestonfield House Hotel (www
  .prestonfield.com)
> Scotsman Hotel (www.thescotsman
  hotel.co.uk)
> Witchery by the Castle (www
  .thewitchery.com)

MOST STYLISH HOTELS
> Borough (www.boroughhotel.com)
> Glasshouse (www.theetoncollection
  .com)
> Hotel Missoni (www.hotelmissoni.com)
> Hudson Hotel (www.thehudsonhotel
  .co.uk)
> Tigerlily (www.tigerlilyedinburgh
  .co.uk)

DRINKING

Edinburgh has always been a drinker's city. The 18th-century poets Robert Fergusson and Robert Burns spent much of their time in – and often drew inspiration from – Edinburgh's public houses and, rather than attend his law lectures at Edinburgh University, the young Robert Louis Stevenson preferred to haunt the city's many howffs (drinking dens) – a practice perpetuated by many Edinburgh students to this day.

Although many city-centre pubs have been themed or converted into vast drinking halls catering to office workers unwinding at the end of a day, the neighbourhood bar is still a social centre where you can meet friends, watch football or rugby on TV, listen to live music or take part in the weekly quiz night. Edinburgh has more than 700 pubs – more per square mile than any other UK city – and they are as varied and full of character as the people who drink in them, from Victorian palaces to stylish pre-club bars, and from real-ale howffs to trendy cocktail lounges. Pubs with live music are listed on www.gigguide.co.uk.

During the 19th century, Edinburgh ranked alongside Munich, Pilsen and Burton-on-Trent in importance as a brewing centre, and in the early 1900s laid claim to 28 breweries. Today, there are only two working breweries – Caledonian (now part-owned by Scottish and Newcastle) and Stewart's. Happily, this pair produce some of the finest beers in Britain, including Deuchar's IPA (available in most of the city's real-ale pubs) and Stewart's Edinburgh Gold.

The pubs along the Royal Mile are aimed mainly at the tourist market, but there are still some good old-fashioned drinking dens hidden up the closes and along the side streets. Over in the New Town, you'll find many of the city's most fashionable cocktail bars on or near George St, while neighbouring Rose St was once a famous pub-crawl route, where generations of students, sailors and rugby fans would try to visit every pub on the street (around 17 of them) and down a pint of beer in each one.

BEST TRADITIONAL DECOR
> Abbotsford (p89)
> Bennet's Bar (p121)
> Café Royal Circle Bar (p90)
> Guildford Arms (p91)
> Kay's Bar (p91)

MOST STYLISH COCKTAIL BARS
> Amicus Apple (p89)
> Bramble (p90)
> Sygn (p106)
> Tigerlily (p92)
> Tonic (p93)

BEST LIVE MUSIC BARS
> Ghillie Dhu (p105)
> Royal Oak (p62)
> Sandy Bell's (p63)
> Whistle Binkie's (p63)
> White Hart Inn (p60)

BEST OUTDOOR DRINKING
> Beehive Inn (p59)
> Cumberland Bar (p90)
> Oloroso Lounge Bar (p92)
> Pear Tree House (p123)
> Teuchters Landing (p131)

FOOD

Eating out in Edinburgh has changed beyond all recognition in the last 20 years. Two decades ago, sophisticated dining meant a visit to the Aberdeen Angus Steak House for a prawn cocktail, steak (well done) and chips, and Black Forest gateau, all washed down with a bottle Mateus Rosé. Today, eating out has become a commonplace event and the city can boast more restaurants per head of population than any other city in the UK, including a couple of Michelin stars in the shape of 21212 (p83), Restaurant Martin Wishart (p133) and the Kitchin (p132).

Scotland has never been celebrated for its national cuisine – in fact, from haggis and porridge to deep-fried Mars Bars, it has more often been an object of ridicule. Traditional Scottish cookery was all about basic comfort food – solid, nourishing fare, often high in fat, that would keep you warm on a winter's day. But a new culinary style known as Modern Scottish has emerged in the last 20 years or so.

It's a style that should be familiar to fans of Californian Cuisine and Mod Oz. Chefs take top-quality Scottish produce – from Highland venison, Aberdeen Angus beef and freshly landed seafood, to root vegetables, raspberries and Ayrshire cheeses – and prepare it simply, in a way that enhances the natural flavours, often adding a French, Italian or Asian twist.

As well as this home-grown style, you'll find a wide range of ethnic cuisines on offer, from Turkish to Thai, and with an increasing number of Polish immigrants arriving in the city, places like Bigos (p83) are sure to be joined by more Eastern European eateries.

In addition, most pubs, wine bars and cocktail bars serve food, offering either bar meals or a more formal restaurant, or both. Some, such as the Caley Sample Room (p122), Joseph Pearce's (p91) and Ecco Vino (p59), are every bit as good as dedicated restaurants.

If you want even more listings than we can provide here, the excellent *Edinburgh & Glasgow Eating & Drinking Guide* (www.list.co.uk/ead), published annually by *List* magazine, contains reviews of around 800 restaurants, cafes and bars.

The www.5pm.co.uk website lists last-minute offers from restaurants with tables to spare that evening. Using this service you can find a three-course dinner at one of Edinburgh's better restaurants for as little as £15 if you're prepared to eat early or late.

BEST BREAKFASTS
> Always Sunday (p52)
> Blue Moon Café (p83)
> Diner 7 (p132)
> Jasper's (p118)
> Valvona & Crolla Caffè Bar (p88)

BEST VEGETARIAN
> Ann Purna (p117)
> David Bann (p53)
> Henderson's Salad Table (p85)
> Kalpna (p118)
> L'Artichaut (p86)

BEST MODERN SCOTTISH
> Kitchin (p132)
> Number One (p87)
> Restaurant Martin Wishart (p133)
> Sweet Melindas (p120)
> Tower (p57)

BEST LATE-NIGHT MUNCHIES
> David Bann (p53)
> Ghillie Dhu (p105)
> Gordon's Trattoria (p54)
> Kebab Mahal (p118)
> Thai Lemongrass (p120)

ARCHITECTURE

Edinburgh's unique beauty arises from a combination of its unusual site, perched among craggy hills, and a legacy of fine architecture dating from the 16th century to the present day. The New Town remains the world's most complete and unspoilt example of Georgian architecture and town planning. Along with the Old Town, it was declared a Unesco World Heritage Site in 1995.

One of the outstanding features of the Old Town is the biggest concentration of surviving 17th-century buildings in Britain; these tenements, six to eight stories in height, were among the tallest in Britain. You can explore the interior of a 17th-century tenement at Gladstone's Land (p42) and John Knox House (p44).

Robert Adam (1728–92), one of the leading architects of the 18th century, made his mark in Edinburgh's New Town with neoclassical masterpieces such as Charlotte Sq, Edinburgh University's Old College and Hopetoun House (p129). You can experience the elegance of Adam's interiors by visiting the Georgian House (p73).

The plan for the New Town was the result of a competition won by James Craig, then an unknown, self-taught 23-year-old. At the end of the 20th century another architectural competition resulted in the relatively unknown Enric Miralles being chosen as the architect for the new Scottish Parliament Building. Though its construction was shrouded with controversy, the new building won the 2005 Stirling Prize for the best new architecture in Britain, and has revitalised a near-derelict industrial site at the foot of the Royal Mile.

TOP MODERN ARCHITECTURE
> Glasshouse (p139)
> National Museum of Scotland (p44)
> Ocean Terminal (p131)
> Scottish Parliament Building (p69)
> Tun (p71)

MOST BEAUTIFUL BUILDINGS
> Charlotte Sq (p73)
> George Heriot's School (p41)
> Parliament Hall (p46)
> Royal Scottish Academy (p78)
> Scott Monument (p78)

Left The new Scottish Parliament Building (p69) **Above** The Royal Scottish Academy (p78)

GAY EDINBURGH

Edinburgh has a small – but perfectly formed – gay and lesbian scene, centred on the area around Broughton St (known affectionately as 'The Pink Triangle') at the eastern end of the New Town. Although it's not as mad, bad and dangerous to know as the Glasgow scene, it has enough pubs and clubs to keep the boozing-and-cruising crowd happy.

Broughton St is the place to head to first. The Blue Moon Café is a great place to meet people during the day, and to pick up the latest news about where's hot and where's not. There are several club nights that are gay or lesbian only, or that attract a large gay contingent, but as club nights and venues change often, it's best to check *ScotsGay* magazine (www.scotsgay.com) or the *List* (www.list.co.uk) for the latest details.

Pride Scotia, the annual celebration of Scotland's gay, lesbian and transgender community, begins with a colourful parade along High St, down The Mound, along Princes St, then down Leith St and Broughton St, followed by lots of eating, drinking and dancing at various venues in the Pink Triangle. It's held in odd-numbered years in Edinburgh, on the last Saturday in June.

In July, the Filmhouse (p106) hosts the London Lesbian and Gay Film Festival On Tour.

BEST GAY CLUBS
> CC Blooms (p93)
> Dare@Cabaret Voltaire (p61)
> Tackno (www.tackno.com) at various venues
> Taste/Fever (www.taste-clubs.com) at various venues

BEST GAY PUBS & CAFÉS
> Blue Moon Café (p83)
> Elbow (p91)
> Regent (p92; pictured above)

KIDS' EDINBURGH

Edinburgh has a multitude of attractions for children, and most things to see and do are child-friendly. Kids under five travel for free on Edinburgh buses, and five- to 15-year-olds pay a flat fare of 70p. However you should be aware that the majority of Scottish pubs, even those that serve bar meals, are forbidden by law to admit children under the age of 14; even in the family-friendly pubs (ie those in possession of a Children's Certificate), under-14s are only admitted between the hours of 11am and 8pm, and only when accompanied by an adult aged 18 or over.

The Edinburgh & Scotland Information Centre (p162) has lots of info on children's events, and you can find the handy guidebook *Edinburgh for Under Fives* in most bookshops. *List* magazine (www.list.co.uk) has a special kids' section listing children's activities and events in and around Edinburgh. The week-long International Children's Festival (www.imagin ate.org.uk) takes place each year in late May/early June.

There are good, safe playgrounds in most Edinburgh parks, including Princes Street Gardens West, Inverleith Park (opposite the Royal Botanic Garden), George V Park (New Town), the Meadows and Bruntsfield Links.

During the Edinburgh and Fringe Festivals there's lots of street theatre for kids, especially on High St and at the foot of The Mound, and in December there's a ferris wheel, an open-air ice rink and fairground rides in Princes Street Gardens.

BEST INDOOR STUFF FOR KIDS
> Edinburgh Castle (p12)
> National Museum of Scotland (p17)
> Our Dynamic Earth (p67)
> Real Mary King's Close (p46)
> Royal Commonwealth Pool (p124)

BEST OUTDOOR STUFF FOR KIDS
> Cramond Village (p128)
> Edinburgh Zoo (p98)
> Greyfriars Bobby (p42)
> Royal Botanic Garden (p98)
> Water of Leith (p99)

VIEWS

Edinburgh is one of Europe's most beautiful cities, draped across a series of rocky hills overlooking the sea. It's a town intimately entwined with its landscape, with buildings and monuments perched atop crags and overshadowed by cliffs – in the words of Robert Louis Stevenson, 'a dream in masonry and living rock'.

From the Old Town's picturesque jumble of medieval tenements piled high along the Royal Mile, its turreted skyline strung between the black, bull-nosed Castle Rock and the russet palisade of Salisbury Crags (pictured below), to the New Town's neat grid of neoclassical respectability, all columns and capitals, porticoes and pediments, the city offers a constantly changing perspective. And it's all small enough to explore easily on foot.

A glance in any souvenir shop will reveal a display of postcards that testify to the city's beauty and to its many viewpoints, both natural and man-made. Part of the pleasure of any visit to Edinburgh is simply soaking up the view, so set aside some time to explore the loftier parts of the city, camera in hand.

BEST VIEWPOINTS

> Arthur's Seat (p66)
> Blackford Hill (p109)
> Calton Hill (p73)
> Outlook Tower & Camera Obscura (p45)
> Scott Monument (p78)

RESTAURANTS WITH THE BEST VIEWS

> A Room in Leith (p131)
> Forth Floor Restaurant & Brasserie (p85)
> Maxie's Bistro (p55)
> Oloroso (p87)
> Tower (p57)

Blowing the bagpipes along the Royal Mile (p14)

HISTORY

HOW EDINBURGH GOT ITS NAME

When the Romans first arrived here, the resident tribe was the Votadini, who had settlements on Castle Rock, Arthur's Seat and Blackford Hill. Little is known about these ancient Britons but it seems likely they were the ancestors of the Gododdin, who are mentioned by the Welsh bard Aneirin in a 7th-century manuscript.

Their 'capital' was called Dun Eiden, which meant 'Fort on the Hill Slope', and almost certainly referred to Castle Rock. The Angles, from the kingdom of Northumbria in northeastern England, defeated the Gododdin and captured Dun Eiden in 638. It is thought that the Angles took the existing Celtic name 'Eiden' and tacked it onto their own Old English word for fort, 'burh', to create the name Edinburgh.

CANMORE KINGS & QUEENS

With his Saxon queen, Margaret, Malcolm III Canmore (r 1057–93) founded a solid dynasty of able Scottish rulers. They had their main home in Dunfermline but regularly commuted to the castle at Edinburgh, crossing the Firth of Forth at the Queen's Ferry (now Queensferry, p129).

Until this period there was no record of a town at Edinburgh – just the castle – but from the 11th century a settlement grew along the ridge to the east of Castle Rock. Malcolm's son, David I, held court at the castle and built a church in honour of his mother; today St Margaret's Chapel is the city's oldest surviving building (p12).

A MEDIEVAL MANHATTAN

By the mid-15th century Edinburgh was the de facto royal capital and the political centre of Scotland. The coronation of James II (r 1437–60) was held in the abbey at Holyrood (p67) and the Scottish Parliament met in the Tolbooth on High St or in the castle. The city's first effective town wall was constructed at about this time, enclosing the Old Town. This overcrowded area – by then the most populous town in Scotland – became a medieval Manhattan, forcing its densely packed inhabitants to build upwards instead of outwards, creating tenements that towered up to eight storeys high.

RENAISSANCE KING

James IV (r 1488–1513) of Scotland married the daughter of Henry VII of England, the first of the Tudor monarchs, thereby uniting the two royal families through 'the Marriage of the Thistle and the Rose'. James was a true Renaissance man, interested in science, technology and the arts, and his reign was a golden era that saw Edinburgh Castle become one of Britain's biggest gun foundries, the establishment of a supreme law court and the creation of a Scottish navy. Much graceful Scottish architecture dates from this time, and the Renaissance style can be seen in the alterations and additions made to the royal Palace of Holyroodhouse (p68).

THE KILLING TIME

In the 16th century the Reformation tore through Scotland. The hellfire preaching of John Knox, a pupil of the Swiss reformer Calvin, found sympathetic ears in Edinburgh – Knox was the minister at St Giles Cathedral (p46) – and in 1560 the Scottish Parliament created a Protestant church that was independent of Rome and of the monarchy.

The 17th century was a time of civil war. Attempts by Charles I to impose the rule of bishops on Scotland ignited public riots in Edinburgh – the Presbyterian Scottish Church believed in a personal bond with God that saw no need for mediation through priests and bishops, and in 1638 hundreds gathered in Greyfriars Kirkyard (p43) to sign the National Covenant, a declaration affirming their rights and beliefs. Scotland became divided between the Covenanters and those who supported the king.

Although the Scots opposed Charles I's religious beliefs, they were appalled when Oliver Cromwell's parliamentarians executed the king in 1649. They offered his son Charles II (r 1649–85) the Scottish crown as long as he signed the Covenant, which he did. But following his restoration in 1660, the king reneged on the Covenant, and his successor, James VII of Scotland/II of England (r 1685–89) made worshipping as a Covenanter a capital offence. This period, during which the Covenanters endured relentless persecution, came to be known as 'the killing time' – around 1200 Covenanters were incarcerated in appalling conditions in a corner of Greyfriars Kirkyard, still known today as the Covenanters Prison.

UNION WITH ENGLAND

By the end of the 17th century, Edinburgh was indisputably Scotland's most important city. Civil war had left the country and its economy ruined, however, and it became clear to wealthy Scottish merchants that the only way to make money in the lucrative markets of developing

V

BACKGROUND

colonies was through union with England. Despite public opposition, the Act of Union – which brought the two countries under one parliament, one sovereign and one flag, but preserved the independence of the Scottish Church and legal system – took effect on 1 May 1707.

A HOTBED OF GENIUS

Although Edinburgh declined in political importance following the removal of the Scottish Parliament in 1707, its cultural and intellectual life flourished. During the period that came to be called the Scottish Enlightenment (roughly 1740–1830) Edinburgh was known as a hotbed of genius, famed throughout Europe for its great philosophers, scientists and artists.

Edinburgh was home to philosopher David Hume, author of the influential *Treatise on Human Nature,* and political economist Adam Smith,

THE RESURRECTION MEN

In 1505 Edinburgh's newly founded Royal College of Surgeons was officially allocated the corpse of one executed criminal per year for the purposes of dissection. But this was not nearly enough to satisfy the curiosity of the city's anatomists, and an illegal trade in dead bodies emerged. The trade culminated in the early 19th century when the anatomy classes of famous surgeons, such as Professor Robert Knox, drew audiences of up to 500 people.

The readiest supply of corpses was to be found in the city's graveyards, especially Greyfriars (p43). Grave robbers – or 'resurrection men' – plundered newly interred coffins and sold the cadavers to the anatomists, who turned a blind eye to the source of their research material.

The notorious William Burke and William Hare, who lived near the Grassmarket, took the body-snatching business a step further. When an elderly lodger died without paying his rent, Burke and Hare sold his body to the famous Professor Knox. Seeing a lucrative business opportunity they figured that, rather than waiting for someone else to die, they could create their own supply of fresh cadavers by resorting to murder.

Burke and Hare preyed on the poor and weak of Edinburgh's Grassmarket, luring them back to Hare's lodging house, plying them with drink and then suffocating their victims. Between December 1827 and October 1828 they murdered at least 16 people, selling their bodies to Professor Knox. When the law finally caught up with them, Hare turned King's evidence and testified against Burke.

Burke was hanged outside St Giles Kirk in January 1829 and, in an ironic twist, his body was given to the anatomy school for public dissection. His skeleton and a wallet made from his skin are still on display in the Surgeons' Hall Museums (p109).

who wrote *The Wealth of Nations*. Publisher William Smellie established the Encyclopedia Britannica, and architect Robert Adam emerged as Britain's greatest exponent of neoclassicism.

WORLD HERITAGE SITE

Although the Industrial Revolution affected Edinburgh on a much smaller scale than it did Glasgow, it brought many changes. Ironworks, potteries, glass factories and light engineering were added to the traditional industries of baking, brewing, distilling and publishing. During the 19th century Edinburgh's population quadrupled in size to 400,000 – not much less than it is today.

Following WWII the city's cultural life blossomed, stimulated by the Edinburgh International Festival (p25) and its fellow traveller the Fringe (p25), both held for the first time in 1947. The University of Edinburgh established itself as a teaching and research centre of international importance in areas such as medicine, electronics and artificial intelligence.

Poorly planned redevelopment in the 1960s and '70s resulted in the demolition of large parts of the city centre and the construction of various concrete monstrosities, notably the St James Centre at the eastern end of Princes St. Fortunately, not all of the plans were realised, and Edinburgh was spared the horror of a motorway running the length of Princes Street Gardens. In 1995 both the Old and New Towns were declared Unesco World Heritage Sites.

THERE SHALL BE A SCOTTISH PARLIAMENT

From 1979 to 1997, Scotland was ruled by a Conservative government in London for which the majority of Scots hadn't voted. Separatist feelings, always present, grew stronger. Following the landslide victory of the Labour Party in May 1997, a referendum was held over the creation of a Scottish Parliament – the result was overwhelmingly and unambiguously in favour.

The opening clause of the *Scotland Act 1998* declared, 'There shall be a Scottish Parliament', and the Labour government was true to its word. The new Parliament was officially opened by Queen Elizabeth II on 1 July 1999. However, it wasn't until October 2004 that the Parliament was able to move into its controversial new home in Holyrood (p69) at the foot of the Royal Mile.

LIFE AS AN EDINBURGHER

Edinburgh was once portrayed as a prim Presbyterian city full of repressed Calvinists who would no sooner speak to a stranger in the street than they would punch a church minister in the mouth. Today, however, Edinburgh is the most cosmopolitan city in Scotland – it's often described as the 'least Scottish' of Scottish cities; anyone who lives here for any length of time soon finds out that many of the people they meet are not native Edinburghers.

This cosmopolitan blend means that there is no longer any such thing as a 'typical' Edinburgh resident…except, perhaps, in the mind of Glaswegians, who will be happy to tell you – often at great length – that their east-coast neighbours are smug, superior, stuck-up and standoffish.

The old Edinburgh stereotype was the blue-rinsed and handbagged Morningside lady who spent her days drinking tea with her friends, shopping at Jenners for tweeds and twinsets, and twitching the lace curtains in the front room to keep an eye on the neighbours. The annual Festival Fringe was an occasion for writing letters of complaint to the *Scotsman* and 'sex' was what the coalman delivered your coal in.

The Morningside ladies still exist – keep your eyes and ears open in Jenners – but today the typical young professional Edinburgher probably lives in a tenement flat or modern apartment (paid for with a hefty mortgage), works in financial services and spends far too much time each evening circling the block in the eternal quest for a parking space. They drink wine rather than beer, latte rather than tea, and eat out at least once a week. They're obsessed with property prices, take a week or two's skiing holiday each winter and dream about owning a farmhouse in France.

All the same, living in Edinburgh has many benefits. The place is small enough to have a human scale, and you're forever bumping into people you know – someone once said that Edinburgh is a city the size of a town that feels like a village, and you'll soon see what they mean. Its compact size means that getting around is easy, and the countryside is never more than half an hour away. You can go walking through the Pentland Hills or sailing on the Firth of Forth – both are only a few miles from the city centre – and the Scottish Highlands are only an hour's drive to the north.

DID YOU KNOW?
> Population: 477,660
> Inflation: 3.1%
> Unemployment: 3.6%
> Average annual income: £26,848
> Average house price: £212,000

GOVERNMENT & POLITICS

Despite the global financial crisis, Edinburgh still has a spring in its step. The presence of the Scottish Parliament and the fast-recovering financial sector in the city have seen lower unemployment and higher average income and higher property prices than in the rest of the country. And there are plenty of politicians in Edinburgh, both in the Scottish Parliament and on the City of Edinburgh Council, who are trying to take the credit for all this.

The Scottish Parliament is a single-chamber system with 129 members (known as MSPs), who are elected through proportional representation and led by a first minister, currently Alex Salmond. The parliament sits for four-year terms and is responsible for so-called 'devolved matters': education, health, housing, transport, economic development and other domestic affairs. It also has the power (as yet this has not been used) to increase or decrease the rate of income tax in Scotland by up to 3%. Westminster, however, still has power over so-called 'reserved matters', such as defence, foreign affairs and social security.

In contrast to Westminster (where the main political contest is between the Labour and Conservative parties, with the Liberal Democrats coming third), Scotland has four main political parties – the Labour Party, the Scottish National Party (SNP), the Scottish Conservative and Unionist Party, and the Liberal Democrats (Lib Dems). The main struggle for political power in Scotland is between the Labour party and the SNP.

Edinburgh's local government is in the hands of the City of Edinburgh Council, based in the City Chambers in High St. The council is popularly elected and serves four-year terms.

FURTHER READING

Edinburgh has always been at the heart of the Scottish literary scene, from the classical works of Robert Burns, Sir Walter Scott and Robert Louis Stevenson to the modern 'brat pack' of Iain Banks, Irvine Welsh, Ian Rankin and Christopher Brookmyre. There are countless novels in which the city is the star.

44 Scotland Street (Alexander McCall Smith, 2004) Beginning as a serialised novel in the *Scotsman* newspaper, these absorbing, humorous and elegantly interwoven stories of the inhabitants of neighbouring New Town flats have now extended to a third volume.

Born Free (Laura Hird, 1999) Bringing vividly to life an aspect of the city that tourists never see, this is a gritty and tragic but heart-warming tale of modern family life in one of Edinburgh's poorer neighbourhoods.

Complicity (Iain Banks, 1993) A gruesome and often hilarious thriller-cum-satire on the greed and corruption of the Thatcher years as it follows a strung-out journalist on the trail of a serial killer through the backdrop of Edinburgh.

The Falls (Ian Rankin, 2001) A gripping noir-style crime novel that stars hard-drinking detective John Rebus, Edinburgh's answer to Sam Spade, as he struggles to solve the disappearance of a student while grappling with shades of the city's dark history.

Fleshmarket (Nicola Morgan, 2003) Aimed primarily at a teenage readership, this is a gory tale of revenge and redemption set in early-19th-century Edinburgh that follows the adventures of a boy who gets mixed up in the murky world of the notorious body-snatchers Burke and Hare (p152).

The Heart of Midlothian (Sir Walter Scott, 1818) Perhaps Scott's finest and most complex work, this novel is set in Edinburgh in the first half of the 18th century and deals with justice, and the lack of it, seen through the eyes of Jeanie Deans, a heroine far ahead of her time.

The Prime of Miss Jean Brodie (Muriel Spark, 1962) The story of a charismatic teacher in a 1930s Edinburgh girls' school who leads her chosen girls – her *crème de la crème* – in the pursuit of truth and beauty, with devastating consequences.

The Private Memoirs and Confessions of a Justified Sinner (James Hogg, 1824) This post-modern novel was some 150 years ahead of its time and is both a murder story told from two points of view and an ingenious deconstruction of the religious certainties of 18th-century Scotland.

Skinner's Rules (Quintin Jardine, 1993) The first in a series of well-plotted detective stories centred on Edinburgh CID chief Bob Skinner; not as dark or as satisfying as Ian Rankin's Rebus novels, but gripping nonetheless.

Trainspotting (Irvine Welsh, 1993) A disturbing and darkly humorous journey through the junkie underworld of 1990s Edinburgh, pulling no punches as it charts hero Renton's descent into heroin addiction.

DIRECTORY

TRANSPORT
ARRIVAL & DEPARTURE
AIR
Edinburgh Airport (code EDI; ☎ 0131-333 1000; www.edinburghairport.com) is 8 miles west of the city. It has a tourist information and accommodation desk, left-luggage facilities, ATMs, currency-exchange desks, shops, restaurants, internet access and car-hire agencies.

BUS
Edinburgh bus station (Map p74-5), the terminus for regional and long-distance bus services, is at the northeast corner of St Andrew Sq, with pedestrian entrances from the square and from Elder St. There are information desks, internet access and left-luggage facilities. For timetable information, contact **Traveline** (☎ 0871 200 2233; www.travelinescotland.com). It's worth checking **Megabus** (☎ 0900 160 0900; www.megabus.com) for cheap inter-city bus fares (from as little as £3) to Edinburgh from major English cities.

TRAIN
The main terminus in Edinburgh is **Waverley train station** (Map p74-5, E5; Waverley Bridge), located in the heart of the city. Trains arriving from, and departing to, the west also stop at **Haymarket train station** (Map p97, D4; Haymarket Tce), which is more convenient for the West End. You can buy tickets, make reservations and get travel information at the **Edinburgh Rail Travel Centre** (Map p74-5; Waverley train station, Waverley Bridge; ⏱ 4.45am-12.30am Mon-Sat, 7am-12.30am Sun) in Waverley station. For fare and timetable enquires, phone the **National Rail Enquiry Service**

GETTING INTO TOWN FROM EDINBURGH AIRPORT

	Airlink Bus 100	Taxi
Pick-up point	Coach Park outside terminal building	taxi rank outside terminal building
Drop-off point	Haymarket, West End, Waverley train station	anywhere
Duration	30min	to centre, 15-20min
Cost	single/return £3/6	to centre, £14-15
Frequency	runs every 10min	n/a
Contact	☎ 0131 555 6363; www.flyybus.com	☎ 0131 333 2255

(☎ 0845 748 4950) or check the timetables at www.scotrail.co.uk or www.nationalrail.co.uk. Buy tickets online at www.thetrainline.com.

GETTING AROUND

Until a new tram system is installed (scheduled to be running by 2011), public transport within Edinburgh is provided entirely by buses. In this book, the best bus routes are noted after the 🚌 in each listing.

BUS

The two main operators are **Lothian Buses** (☎ 555 6363; www.lothianbuses.co.uk), which runs most of the city routes, and **First Edinburgh** (☎ 663 9233; www.firstedinburgh.co.uk), whose buses mainly serve the towns and villages around Edinburgh. You can get timetable information and

route maps from the offices listed below. Bus timetables, route maps and fare guides are also posted at all main bus stops.

Adult fares within the city are £1.20; children aged under five travel free and those aged five to 15 years pay a flat fare of 70p. On Lothian buses you must pay the driver the exact fare, but First Edinburgh buses will give change. Lothian Buses also offers a Daysaver ticket (£3) that gives unlimited travel (on Lothian Buses only, and excluding night buses) for a day; buy it from the driver. Night buses (www.nightbuses.com), which run hourly between midnight and 5am, charge a flat fare of £3.

First Edinburgh Bus Shop (Map p74-5, D4; Edinburgh bus station; ◷ 8.30am-6pm Mon-Sat, 9.30am-5pm Sun)

Lothian Buses Travel Shop New Town (Map p74-5, D5; Waverley Bridge; ◷ 8.30am-6pm Mon-Sat, 9.30am-5pm Sun); New Town (Map

TRANSPORT AROUND EDINBURGH

	High St, Royal Mile	Scottish Parliament	George St	Stockbridge	Leith
High St, Royal Mile	n/a	walk 15min	walk 15min	bus 10min	bus 20min
Scottish Parliament	walk 15min	n/a	walk 15min	bus 20min	bus 20min
George St	walk 15min	walk 15min	n/a	walk 10min	bus 20min
Stockbridge	bus 10min	bus 20min	walk 10min	n/a	bus 20min
Leith	bus 20min	bus 20min	bus 20min	bus 20min	n/a

p74-5, C5; 27 Hanover St; ⊗ 8.30am-6pm
Mon-Sat); West End (Map p97, E3; 7-9 Shandwick Pl; ⊗ 8.30am-6pm Mon-Sat)

GREENER WAYS TO EDINBURGH

Flying from Edinburgh to London may be cheap, but when you take into account the time
and expense of getting to your departure airport, taking the train all the way begins to look
like a more attractive option. The fastest trains take only four hours from Kings Cross to
Waverley, and if you travel on a weekday there's the option of spending most of the journey
in the restaurant car enjoying a three-course meal and a bottle of wine. Book far enough in
advance and the fare can be as little as £60 return, though £100 is more realistic. Check out
the UK train travel section of www.seat61.com.

TAXI

Edinburgh's black taxis can be
hailed in the street, ordered by
phone (extra 80p charge), or picked
up at one of the many central ranks.
The minimum charge is £1.60 (£2.70
at night) for the first 450m, then 25p
for every subsequent 210m or 45
seconds – a typical 2-mile trip across
the city centre will cost around £6.
Tipping is up to you – because of
the high fares local people rarely tip
on short journeys, but occasionally
round up to the nearest 50p on
longer ones.

Central Taxis (☎ 229 2468)
City Cabs (☎ 228 1211)
ComCab (☎ 272 8000)

PRACTICALITIES
BUSINESS HOURS

Banks 9.30am-4pm Mon-Fri, some branches
9.30am-12.30pm Sat
Businesses 9am-5pm Mon-Fri

Post offices 9am-5.30pm Mon-Fri, 9am-
12.30pm Sat
Pubs & bars 11am-11pm Mon-Thu, 11am-
1am Fri & Sat, 12.30-11pm Sun
Restaurants noon-2.30pm & 6-10pm
Shops 9am-5.30pm Mon-Sat, some to 8pm
Thu, 11am-5pm Sun

DISCOUNTS

The Edinburgh Pass (www.edinburgh.org/
pass; one/two/three days £26.50/39/51.50)
offers free entry to more than
30 attractions and tours, plus
unlimited travel on Lothian bus
services and one return journey
on the Airlink 100 airport bus. As
yet, entry to Edinburgh Castle and
the Royal Yacht Britannia are not
included in the pass.

EMERGENCIES

Edinburgh is safer than most cities
of a similar size, but it has its share
of crime so all of the normal big-
city precautions apply here.
   Lothian Rd, Dalry Rd, Rose St
and the western end of Princes St,
at the junction with Shandwick

CLIMATE CHANGE & TRAVEL

Every form of transport that relies on carbon-based fuel generates CO2, the main cause of human-induced climate change. Modern travel is dependent on aeroplanes, which might use less fuel per kilometre per person than most cars but travel much greater distances. The altitude at which aircraft emit gases (including CO2) and particles also contributes to their climate change impact. Many websites offer 'carbon calculators' that allow people to estimate the carbon emissions generated by their journey and, for those who wish to do so, to offset the impact of the greenhouse gases emitted with contributions to portfolios of climate-friendly initiatives throughout the world. Lonely Planet offsets the carbon footprint of all staff and author travel.

Pl and Queensferry and Hope Sts, can get a bit rowdy on Friday and Saturday nights after the pubs close. Calton Hill offers good views during the day but is best avoided at night. Women on their own should avoid walking across the Meadows after dark and walking in the red-light district between Salamander St and Leith Links, in Leith.

In an emergency, dial ☎ 999 or ☎ 112 (no money needed at public phones) and ask for police, ambulance, fire brigade or coastguard. Other useful phone numbers:

Edinburgh Rape Crisis Centre (☎ 556 9437; www.rapecrisisscotland.org.uk)
Lothian & Borders Police HQ (☎ 311 3131; www.lbp.police.uk; Fettes Ave)
Lothian & Borders Police Info Centre (☎ 226 6966; 188 High St; ☺ 10am-10pm May-Aug, 10am-8pm Mar, Apr, Sep & Oct, 10am-6pm Nov-Feb) You can report a crime or make lost-property enquiries here.

HOLIDAYS

New Year's Day 1 January
New Year Bank Holiday 2 January
Spring Bank Holiday Second Monday in April
Good Friday Friday before Easter Sunday
May Day Holiday First Monday in May
Christmas Day 25 December
Boxing Day 26 December

Edinburgh also has its own local holidays on the third Monday in May and the third Monday in September, when post offices and some shops and businesses are closed.

INTERNET

There are dozens of internet cafes (around £2 per hour) and hundreds of wi-fi hotspots in the city. Useful central locations include:

connect@edinburgh (Map p74-5, E5; ☎ 473 3800; Edinburgh & Scotland Information Centre, Princes Mall, 3 Princes St; ☺ 9am-8pm Mon-Sat & 10am-8pm Sun Jul

& Aug, 9am-7pm Mon-Sat & 10am-7pm Sun May, Jun & Sep, 9am-5pm Mon-Wed, 9am-6pm Thu-Sat & 10am-5pm Sun Oct-Apr)
easyInternetcafé (Map p74-5, C5; ☎ 220 3580; www.easy-everything.com; 58 Rose St; ☯ 7.30am-10.30pm)
G-Tec (Map p38; ☎ 629 0098; www.grass market-technologies.com; 67 Grassmarket; ☯ 10am-6pm Mon-Fri, 10am-5.30pm Sat)

Useful websites include:
City of Edinburgh Council (www.edinburgh .gov.uk) The city council's official site, with a useful events guide.
Edinburgh Architecture (www.edinburgh architecture.co.uk) Informative site dedicated to the city's modern architecture.
Edinburgh & Lothians Tourist Board (www.edinburgh.org) Official tourist board site, with listings of accommodation, sights, activities and events.
Events Edinburgh (www.eventsedinburgh .org.uk) The city council's official events guide.
Gig Guide (www.gigguide.co.uk) Listings of live music sessions in Edinburgh pubs.
List (www.list.co.uk) Restaurant and enter-tainment listings and reviews.

MONEY
Edinburgh ain't cheap, so for an easygoing visit without having to worry about watching the pennies, plan on at least £60 a day per person spending money on top of your accommodation costs. On a tight budget, you can get away with £35 a day.

The easiest way to get hold of cash is from the 24-hour ATMs all over the city, where you can use Visa, MasterCard, Amex, Cirrus, Plus and Maestro cards. An increasing number of ATMs (especially ones in shops) charge a fee (about £1.50) for withdrawals, but most are free.

You can change currency and travellers cheques at exchange counters (known as *bureaux de change*), banks, post offices and travel agencies. Banks generally offer the best rates. Be careful using *bureaux de change*; they may offer good exchange rates but frequently levy large commissions and fees.

ORGANISED TOURS
There are plenty of organised tours to explore Edinburgh, by bus or on foot. The following walking tours are particularly recommended:
Black Hart Storytellers (☎ 225 9044; www.blackhart.uk.com; adult/concession £9.50/7.50) Not suitable for young children. The 'City of the Dead' tour of Greyfriars Kirk-yard is probably the best of Edinburgh's ghost tours. Many people have reported encounters with the McKenzie Poltergeist.
Cadies & Witchery Tours (☎ 225 6745; www.witcherytours.com; adult/child £7.50/5) The becloaked and pasty-faced Adam Lyal (deceased) leads a 'Murder & Mystery' tour of the Old Town's darker corners. These tours are famous for their 'jumper-ooters' – costumed actors who 'jump oot' when you least expect it. Very entertaining.
Edinburgh Literary Pub Tour (☎ 226 6665; www.edinburghliterarypubtour.co.uk; adult/ student £10/8) An enlightening two-hour trawl through Edinburgh's literary history – and its associated howffs (drinking dens) – in the en-tertaining company of Messrs Clart and McBrain. One of the best of Edinburgh's walking tours.

Mercat Tours (☎ 557 6464; www.mercat tours.com; adult/child £9/5) Mercat offers a wide range of fascinating tours, including history walks in the Old Town and Leith, 'Ghosts & Ghouls' tours and visits to haunted underground vaults.

Rebus Tours (☎ 553 7473; www .rebustours.com; adult/concession £10/9; ☺ Sat only) These two-hour guided walking tours themed on Ian Rankin's Inspector Rebus novels take you off the beaten tourist trail and into some unlikely corners of the city. Bookings are essential.

TELEPHONE

The UK uses the GSM 900/1800 network, which is compatible with the rest of Europe, Australia and New Zealand, but not with the North American GSM 1900 system or the totally different system used in Japan (though some North Americans have GSM 1900/900 phones that will work in the UK). Make sure your phone has roaming capability before you leave home. Alternatively, there are plenty of public phones in Edinburgh, operated by either coins, phonecards or credit cards; phonecards are available in newsagents.

COUNTRY & CITY CODES
Edinburgh (☎ 0131)
UK (☎ 44)

USEFUL NUMBERS
Directory assistance (☎ 118 118, 118 500)
International access code (☎ 00)

International directory enquiries
(☎ 118 161)
International operator (☎ 155)
Local & national operator (☎ 100)
Reverse-charge/collect calls (☎ 155)
Time (☎ 123)

TIPPING
In general, when you eat in an Edinburgh restaurant you should leave a tip of at least 10% unless the service was unsatisfactory. If the bill already includes a service charge (usually 10%), you needn't add a further tip. Tipping in bars is not customary.

Taxis in Edinburgh are expensive, and drivers rarely expect a tip unless they have gone out of their way to help you.

TOURIST INFORMATION
VisitScotland Edinburgh (www.edinburgh .org) is the city's main provider of tourist information, with an office in the **Edinburgh & Scotland Information Centre** (ESIC; Map p74-5, E5; ☎ 0845-225 5121; Princes Mall, 3 Princes St; ☺ 9am-8pm Mon-Sat & 10am-8pm Sun Jul & Aug, 9am-7pm Mon-Sat & 10am-7pm Sun May, Jun & Sep, 9am-5pm Mon-Wed, 9am-6pm Thu-Sat & 10am-5pm Sun Oct-Apr).

TRAVELLERS WITH DISABILITIES
Edinburgh's Old Town, with its steep hills, narrow closes, flights of stairs and cobbled streets, is a

challenge for wheelchair users. Large new hotels and modern tourist attractions are usually fine; however, many B&Bs and guesthouses are in hard-to-adapt older buildings that lack ramps and lifts. It's a similar story with public transport. Newer buses have steps or suspension that lowers for access, but it's wise to check before setting out. Most black taxis are wheelchair-friendly.

Many banks are fitted with induction loops to assist the hearing impaired. Some attractions have Braille guides for the visually impaired.

VisitScotland produces a guide, *Accessible Scotland,* for travellers with disabilities, and the Edin-burgh & Scotland Information Centre has accessibility details for Edinburgh.

VISAS

Visa regulations are subject to change so it's essential to check before travelling – see www.uk visas.gov.uk or the Lonely Planet (www.lonelyplanet.com) website. Citizens of Australia, Canada, New Zealand, South Africa or the USA can stay for up to six months (no visa required). EU citizens can live and work in Britain free of immigration control and don't need a visa to enter the country. All other nationalities should contact their nearest British diplomatic mission to obtain a visa.

>INDEX

See also separate subindexes for See (p172), Shop (p173), Eat (p174), Drink (p175) and Play (p176).

A

accommodation 138-9
Act of Union 12, 152
Adam, Robert 144
air travel 157
ale 56, 141
ambulance 160
architecture 70, 144-5
Arthur's Seat 66
Arthur's Seat area 64-71, **65**
arts 20
    festivals 10-11, 25
ATMs 161

B

Banks, Iain 156
bars 18, *see also* Drink
    subindex
beer 56, 141
Beltane 24
Blackford Hill 109
boat travel 112, 121, 128, 129
body-snatchers 68, 152
    books 156
books 20, 156
Britannia, Royal Yacht 22, 129
buildings of note, *see* See
    subindex
burial grounds, *see* kirkyards
Burke & Hare 68, 152, 156
Burke, William 68, 152, 156
bus travel 157, 158
business hours 159

000 map pages

C

Calton Hill 73
Camera Obscura 45
canals 112
Canmore dynasty 150
Canongate 15
Canongate Kirk 37
Castle, Edinburgh 12-13, 40-1
Castlehill 15
cathedrals, *see* See *subindex*
cell phones 162
cemeteries, *see* kirkyards
Charlotte Square 73
children, travel with 24, 147
Christmas 26
churches, *see* See *subindex*
cinemas, *see also* Play
    subindex
    New Town 95
    South Edinburgh 124
    West End & Stockbridge 106
City Art Centre 37
City Chambers 37, 40
clubs, *see also* Play *subindex*
    New Town 93, 95
    Old Town 61-3
    South Edinburgh 125
coffins, miniature 68
Collective Gallery 21, 40
comedy, *see also* Play
    subindex
    New Town 95
    Old Town 61
costs 161
    food, *see inside front cover*

D

Da Vinci Code 112
dance, *see* Play *subindex*
Dean Gallery 98
disabilities, travellers with
    162-3
drinking 18, 140-1, *see also*
    ale, beer, whisky, Drink
    subindex
    Leith & the Waterfront
    134-5
    New Town 89-92
    Old Town 58-60
    South Edinburgh 121-4
    West End & Stockbridge
    105-6
Duddingston Parish Church 66
Dunbar's Close Garden 40
Dungeon, Edinburgh 41

E

eating, *see* food
economy 155
Edinburgh Castle 12-13, 40-1
Edinburgh Dungeon 41
Edinburgh Festival Fringe
    10-11, 25
Edinburgh International
    Book Festival 25
Edinburgh International
    Festival 10-11, 25

C

Covenanters 151
Craig, James 145
Cramond village 128
cultural festivals 26

Edinburgh International Film Festival 24
Edinburgh International Jazz & Blues Festival 25
Edinburgh International Science Festival 24
Edinburgh Mela 26
Edinburgh Military Tattoo 25
Edinburgh Pass 159
Edinburgh Printmakers' Workshop & Gallery 73
Edinburgh Zoo 98
emergencies 159-60
Enlightenment, Scottish 152-3
entertainment, see also Play subindex
internet resources 26, 161
events 10-11, 23-6
exchange rates, see inside front cover

F
ferries 128, 129
festivals 10-11, 23-6
film festivals 24
fire services 160
fitness, see health & fitness
Flodden Wall 41
food 142-3, see also Eat subindex
costs, see inside front cover
Holyrood & Arthur's Seat 71
internet resources 143
Leith & the Waterfront 131-4
New Town 83-8
Old Town 52-8
South Edinburgh 117-21

West End & Stockbridge 102-5
Fringe, Edinburgh Festival 10-11, 25
Fruitmarket Gallery 41

G
galleries 21, see also See subindex
Holyrood & Arthur's Seat 68-9
New Town 73, 76, 78-9
Old Town 37, 40, 41, 47-8
West End & Stockbridge 98-9
gardens 19, see also parks, See subindex
New Town 77
Old Town 40
West End & Stockbridge 98
gay travellers 146
George Heriot's School 41
Georgian House 73, 76
ghosts 16, 43
tours 161-2
Gilmerton Cove 109
Gladstone, William 42
Gladstone's Land 42
golf, birthplace of 128
government 155
Graham, James 43
Greyfriars Bobby 42-3
Greyfriars Kirk & Kirkyard 43
gyms, see health & fitness

H
Hare, William 68, 152, 156
haunted places 16, 43
tours 161-2
Hawes Inn 129
health & fitness, see also Play subindex

South Edinburgh 125
West End & Stockbridge 106-7
Heart of Midlothian 43
Heriot, George 41
High St 15
Highland Tolbooth Kirk 43
hiking, see walks
Hird, Laura 156
history 150-6
Hogg, James 156
Hogmanay 26
holidays 160
Holyrood 64-71, **65**
Holyrood Abbey 67
Holyrood Park 66
Holyroodhouse, Palace of 68
Hopetoun House 129
hotels 138-9

I
Inchcolm 128
International Children's Festival 24
International Festival, Edinburgh 10-11, 25
internet access 160-1
internet resources
accommodation 139
children, travel with 147
entertainment 26, 161
food 143
gay & lesbian travellers 146
itineraries 29-31

J
Jardine, Quintin 156
jazz venues, see Play subindex
John Knox House 44

000 map pages

K
killing time, the 151
kirkyards, see also
  See subindex
  New Town 76-7
  Old Town 37, 43
Knights Templar 112
Knox, John 44, 151

L
landmarks, see See subindex
left luggage 157
Leith 126-35, 127
Leith Links 128
lesbian travellers 146
literature 20, 156
  literary festivals 25
  literary tours 161-2
live music, see music venues
lost property 160

M
MacKenzie Poltergeist 16
Maid of the Forth ferry 129
Mansfield Place Church 76
Mary King's Close 16, 46, 47
Mary Queen of Scots 68
McCall Smith, Alexander 156
Meadows, The 109
medieval Edinburgh 150
miniature coffins 68
Miralles, Enric 70, 145
mobile phones 162
money 159, 161
Morgan, Nicola 156
museums, see also See
  subindex
  Holyrood & Arthur's Seat 67
  Leith & the Waterfront
  128-9
  Old Town 17, 44-6
  South Edinburgh 109

music festivals 25
music venues, see also Play
  subindex
  New Town 93
  Old Town 61-3
  South Edinburgh 124
  West End & Stockbridge 107

N
National Gallery of Scotland
  21, 76
National Museum of Scotland
  17, 44-5
National War Museum of
  Scotland 45
Nelson Monument 76
New Town 72-95, 74-5
Newhaven Harbour 128
nightlife, see Play subindex

O
Old Calton Burial Ground 76-7
Old College 45
Old Town 36-63, 38-9
One O'Clock Gun 13, 78
opening hours 159
Outlook Tower 45

P
Palace of Holyroodhouse 68
parks 19, see also gardens,
  See subindex
  Holyrood & Arthur's Seat 66
  Leith & the Waterfront 128
  South Edinburgh 109
  West End & Stockbridge 99
Parliament Hall 46
passes 159
planning 30, 159
police 160
politics 155
population 154

Princes Street Gardens 77
public holidays 160
pubs 18, see also
  Drink subindex
Pugin, Augustus 43

Q
Queen's Gallery 68-9
Queensferry 129
Queensferry Museum 129

R
Rankin, Ian 156
Real Mary King's Close 16,
  46, 47
restaurants, see food,
  Eat subindex
Roman period 150
Roslin 112
Rosslyn Chapel 112
Royal Botanic Garden 98
Royal Highland Show 24
Royal Mile 14-15
Royal Scottish Academy 78
Royal Yacht Britannia 22,
  128-9

S
St Giles Cathedral 46-7
St Margaret's Chapel 12
Scotch Whisky Experience 46
Scotland Act 153
Scott Monument 78
Scott, Sir Walter 78, 156
Scottish Enlightenment 152-3
Scottish International
  Storytelling Festival 26
Scottish National Gallery of
  Modern Art 21, 98-9
Scottish National Portrait
  Gallery 78-9
Scottish Parliament 153

Scottish Parliament Building 69, 70
shopping, *see also*
    Shop *subindex*
    Leith & the Waterfront 130-1
    New Town 79-82
    Old Town 48-52
    South Edinburgh 114-17
    West End & Stockbridge 99-102
Shore, The 129
sights, *see* See *subindex*
sleeping 138-9
South Edinburgh 108-25, **110-11**
Spark, Muriel 156
Stills Gallery 47
Stockbridge 96-107, **97**
Stone of Destiny 40
Surgeons' Hall Museums 109

T
Talbot Rice Gallery 47-8
taxis 159
telephone services 162
theatre, *see also*
    Play *subindex*
    New Town 93
    South Edinburgh 124
    West End & Stockbridge 107
tipping 162
tourist information 162-3
tours 161-2
train travel 157-8, 159
travel passes 159
travellers cheques 161
Trinity House 129-30
Tron Kirk 48

U
underground attractions 16, 47
    Gilmerton Cove 109
Union Canal 112

V
vacations 160
Victorian Royal Museum 17
viewpoints 148, *see also*
    See *subindex*
villages, *see* See *subindex*
visas 163

W
walks
    Holyrood Park 66
    South Edinburgh 109
    Water of Leith Walkway 99
Water of Leith 99
Waterfront, The 126-35, **127**
websites, *see* internet resources
Welsh, Irvine 156
West End 96-107, **97**
whisky 46
Writers' Museum 48

Z
zoos 98

◉ SEE

Boats
Maid of the Forth 129
Royal Yacht Britannia 22, 128-9

Canals
Union Canal 112

Castles
Edinburgh Castle 12-13, 40-1

Churches & Cathedrals
Duddingston Parish Church 66
Greyfriars Kirk & Kirkyard 43
Highland Tolbooth Kirk 43
Mansfield Place Church 76
Rosslyn Chapel 112
St Giles Cathedral 46-7
St Margaret's Chapel 12
Tron Kirk 48

Dungeons
Edinburgh Dungeon 41

Galleries
City Art Centre 37
Collective Gallery 40
Dean Gallery 98
Edinburgh Printmakers' Workshop & Gallery 73
Fruitmarket Gallery 41
National Gallery of Scotland 21, 76
Queen's Gallery 68-9
Scottish National Gallery of Modern Art 21, 98-9
Scottish National Portrait Gallery 78-9
Stills Gallery 47
Talbot Rice Gallery 47-8

Gardens
Dunbar's Close Garden 40
Princes Street Gardens 77
Royal Botanic Garden 98

Islands
Inchcolm 128

Kirkyards
Canongate Kirk 37
Greyfriars Kirk & Kirkyard 43
Old Calton Burial Ground 76-7

000 map pages

Landmarks
Arthur's Seat 66
Calton Hill 73

Museums
Museum of Childhood 44
Museum of Edinburgh 44
Museum on the Mound 44
National Museum of Scotland
   17, 44-5
National War Museum of
   Scotland 45
Our Dynamic Earth 67
Queensferry Museum 129
Royal Yacht Britannia 22,
   128-9
Scotch Whisky Experience
   46
Surgeons' Hall Museums
   109
Victorian Royal Museum 17
Writers' Museum 48

Notable Buildings
Camera Obscura 45
City Chambers 37, 40
George Heriot's School 41
Georgian House 73, 76
Gladstone's Land 42
Hawes Inn 129
Holyrood Abbey 67
Hopetoun House 129
Inchcolm Abbey 128
John Knox House 44
Old College 45
Palace of Holyroodhouse
   68
Parliament Hall 46
Royal Scottish Academy 78
Scottish Parliament Building
   69, 70
Trinity House 129-30

Notable Streets
Real Mary King's Close 16,
   46, 47
Royal Mile 14-15

Palaces
Palace of Holyroodhouse 68

Parks
Blackford Hill 109
Holyrood Park 66
Leith Links 128
Meadows, The 109
Water of Leith 99

Squares
Charlotte Square 73

Statues & Monuments
Greyfriars Bobby 42-3
Heart of Midlothian 43
Nelson Monument 76
Scott Monument 78

Tolbooths
Canongate Tolbooth 37

Viewpoints
Arthur's Seat 66
Blackford Hill 109
Calton Hill 73
Meadows, The 109
Outlook Tower & Camera
   Obscura 45

Villages
Cramond village 128
Queensferry 129

Waterfront Areas
Newhaven Harbour 128
Shore, The 129

Zoos
Edinburgh Zoo 98

SHOP

Antiques
Carson Clark Gallery 49
Courtyard Antiques 115
Edinburgh Architectural
   Salvage Yard 130
Georgian Antiques 131

Arts & Crafts
Adam Pottery 99
Flux 130
Meadows Pottery 116
One World Shop 81
Scottish Gallery 81

Bicycles
Biketrax 114

Books
Blackwell's Bookshop 49
McNaughtan's Bookshop 80
Second Edition 101
Waterstone's 82
West Port Books 116
Word Power 117

Cosmetics
Jo Malone 80

Department Stores
Harvey Nichols 79-80
Jenners 80

Fashion
Arkangel 100
Armstrong's 48
Bill Baber 49
Cookie 50
Corniche 49-50
Cruise 79
Designs on Cashmere 50
Forbidden Planet 50

Geoffrey (Tailor) Inc 50-1
Godiva 51
Greensleeves 115
Joyce Forsyth Designer
  Knitwear 51
Kinross cashmere 51
Liberation 50
Route One 50
Sam Thomas 101
Whiplash Trash 50
Whistles 82

Food & Drink
Crombie's 79
Edinburgh Farmers Market
  100
Fudge House of Edinburgh 50
Ian Mellis 51, 101
Peckham's 116
Royal Mile Whiskies 52
Valvona & Crolla 82

Gay & Lesbian Goods
Q-Store 81

Gifts
Aha Ha Ha 48
Bliss 100
Galerie Mirages 100
Helen Bateman 100
Kiss the Fish 101
Mr Wood's Fossils 51

Glasses
Oscar & Fitch 81

Jewellery
Annie Smith 99-100
Lime Blue 80
Ocean 101
Palenque 51-2

Lingerie
Boudiche 79

Malls
Ocean Terminal 131

Maps
Carson Clark Gallery 49

Markets
Edinburgh Farmers Market
  100

Music
Avalanche Records 49
Backbeat 114
Fopp 79
Hogs Head 115
Mcalister Matheson Music
  101
Underground Solush'n 52

Scottish Goods
Kilberry Bagpipes 115
Kinloch Anderson 131

Shopping Streets
Cockburn Street 50

Sporting Goods
Boardwise 114-15
Tiso 81
Tiso Outdoor Experience
  131

Toys
Aha Ha Ha 48
Mr Wood's Fossils 51
Wonderland 101-2

🍴 EAT

American
Buffalo Grill 102, 117
Katie's Diner 118

Asian
Kebab Mahal 118

Bistros
Café Hub 53
Orocco Pier 129
Urban Angel 88

British
The Dogs 88

Cafes
Always Sunday 52
Blue Moon Café 83
Cafe Newton 103
Café Truva 131-2
caféteria@thefruitmarket 53
Circle 84
Diner 7 132
Foodies at Holyrood 71
Forest Café 53
Fruitmarket Gallery Cafe 54
Jasper's 118
Mum's 55
Valvona & Crolla Caffè Bar 88

Chinese
Chop Chop 103
New Edinburgh Rendezvous
  104
Rainbow Arch 104

French
21212 83
Café Marlayne 53, 83
Café Royal Oyster Bar 83-4
Daniel's Bistro 132
Escargot Blanc 103
Escargot Bleu 84
Grain Store 54-5
Hadrian's Brasserie 85
La P'tite Folie 86, 103-4
Petit Paris 57, 104

Restaurant Martin Wishart 133
Vintners Rooms 134
Witchery by the Castle 58
Zazou 120-1

Fusion
Howie's 85-6

Indian
Kalpna 118
Khushi's 55
Mosque Kitchen 119
Omar Khayyam 104
Roti 119
Suruchi 120

International
Dome Grill Room 84
First Coast 117
Maison Bleue 55
Maxie's Bistro 55

Italian
Centotre 84
Gordon's Trattoria 54
Locanda de Gusti 87
Valvona & Crolla Caffè Bar 88
Valvona & Crolla Vincaffè 88-9

Japanese
Sushiya 120

Mediterranean
Channings Restaurant 103

Mexican
Pancho Villa's 57

Mongolian
Khublai Khan 132

Polish
Bigos 83

Scottish
A Room in Leith 131
Amber 52
Blue 102
Channings Restaurant 103
Doric Tavern 53
First Coast 117
Forth Floor Restaurant & Brasserie 85
Grain Store 54-5
Hadrian's Brasserie 85
Howie's 85-6
Kitchin 132-3
McKirdy's Steakhouse 119
North Bridge Brasserie 55
Number One 87
Oloroso 87
Point Restaurant 119
Restaurant Martin Wishart 133
Rhubarb 71
Stac Polly 87-8
Sweet Melindas 120
Tower 57
Witchery by the Castle 58
Zazou 120-1

Seafood
Café Royal Oyster Bar 83-4
Fishers Bistro 132
Fishers in the City 85
Loch Fyne 133
Mussel Inn 87
Ondine 57
Shore 133-4

Thai
Leven's 118-19
Songkran 104
Songkran II 105
Thai Lemongrass 120

Turkish
Nargile 86-7

Vegetarian
Ann Purna 117
Black Bo's 52
David Bann 53
Engine Shed 117
Henderson's Salad Table 85
L'Artichaut 86

Y DRINK

Bars
Assembly Bar 58
Basement 89-90
Brauhaus 121-2
Elbow 91
Indigo Yard 106
Villager 60

Cafe-Bars
Roseleaf 135

Cocktail Bars
Amicus Apple 89
Bramble 90
Dragonfly 123
Oloroso Lounge Bar 92
Sygn 106
Tigerlily 92-3
Tonic 93

Pubs
Abbotsford 89
Antiquary 105
Auld Hoose 121
Avoca Bar 105
Bailie Bar 105
Beehive Inn 59
Bennet's Bar 121
Bert's Bar 105
Blue Blazer 121

Bow Bar 59
Café Royal Circle Bar 90
Caley Sample Room 122
Canny Man's 122-3
Carriers Quarters 134
Cask & Barrel 90
Clark's Bar 90
Cloisters 123
Cumberland Bar 90
Ghillie Dhu 105
Guildford Arms 91
Jolly Judge 59
Joseph Pearce's 91
Kay's Bar 91
Kenilworth 91
Malt Shovel 59
Mathers 92
Old Chain Pier 134
Oxford Bar 92
Pear Tree House 123
Port O'Leith 135
Regent 92
Robertsons 37 92
Royal Mile Tavern 59-60
Sheep Heid 71
Southsider 123
Starbank Inn 135
White Hart Inn 60

Wine Bars
Ecco Vino 59

⭐ PLAY
Cinemas
Cameo 123-4
Dominion 124
Filmhouse 106
Vue Cinema 95

Clubs
Bongo Club 61
Cabaret Voltaire 61
Caves 61
CC Blooms 93
Liquid Room 62
Lulu 93
Opal Lounge 95
Opium 62
Red Vodka Club 62
Stereo 124-5
Studio 24 63
Voodoo Rooms 95
Wee Red Bar 125

Comedy Clubs
Bedlam Theatre 61
Stand Comedy Club 95

Dance
Dance Base 61
Edinburgh Festival Theatre 124

Folk Music Venues
Pleasance Cabaret Bar 62
Royal Oak 62-3
Sandy Bell's 63

Health & Fitness
Glenogle Swim Centre 107
One Spa 107
Royal Commonwealth Pool 124
Skindulgence 107

Jazz Venues
Jazz Bar 62

Live Music
Jam House 93
Liquid Room 62
Queen's Hall 124
Usher Hall 107
Voodoo Rooms 95
Whistle Binkie's 63

Opera
Edinburgh Festival Theatre 124

Theatres
Edinburgh Festival Theatre 124
Edinburgh Playhouse 93
King's Theatre 124
Royal Lyceum Theatre 107
Traverse Theatre 107

000 map pages